U.S. Human Spaceflight

A RECORD OF ACHIEVEMENT, 1961 – 2006

Compiled by Judith A. Rumerman
Updated by Chris Gamble
and Gabriel Okolski

NASA History Division
Office of External Relations
NASA Headquarters
Washington, DC 20546

Monographs in Aerospace History, No. 41
December 2007
SP-2007-4541

IN MEMORIAM

Apollo 1 (27 January 1967)

Virgil I. "Gus" Grissom • Roger B. Chaffee • Edward H. White II

Portrait of the Apollo 1 prime crew for the first crewed Apollo spaceflight.
(Left to right) Astronauts Edward H. White II, Virgil I. Grissom, and Roger B. Chaffee. (S66-30236)

Challenger, STS-51L (28 January 1986)

Francis R. "Dick" Scobee • Michael J. Smith
Judith A. Resnik • Ellison S. Onizuka • Ronald E. McNair
Gregory B. Jarvis • Sharon Christa McAuliffe

Official portrait of the STS-51L crew members. In the back row (left to right) are mission specialist Ellison S. Onizuka, Teacher in Space participant Sharon Christa McAuliffe, payload specialist Greg Jarvis, and mission specialist Judy Resnik. In the front row are (left to right) pilot Mike Smith, commander Dick Scobee, and mission specialist Ron McNair. (S8544253)

Columbia, STS-107 (1 February 2003)

Rick D. Husband • William C. McCool • Michael P. Anderson
David M. Brown • Kalpana Chawla • Laurel B. Clark
Ilan Ramon (Israel)

The seven STS-107 crew members take a break from their training regimen to pose for the traditional crew portrait. Seated in front (left to right) are astronauts Rick D. Husband, mission commander; Kalpana Chawla, mission specialist; and William C. McCool, pilot. Standing (left to right) are astronauts David M. Brown, Laurel B. Clark, and Michael P. Anderson, all mission specialists, and Ilan Ramon, payload specialist representing the Israeli Space Agency. (GPN-2003-00070)

Library of Congress Cataloging-in-Publication Data

U.S. Human spaceflight : a record of achievement, 1961-2006 /
compiled by Judith A. Rumerman ; updated by Chris Gamble and Gabriel Okolski.
       p. cm.—(Monograph in aerospace history ; no. 41)
  Rev. ed. of: U.S. human spaceflight. 1998.
  Includes bibliographical references and index.
  1. Astronautics—United States—History—Chronology. 2. Space flights—History—Chronology.
3. Manned space flight--History--Chronology. I. Rumerman, Judy A. II. Gamble, Chris. III. Okolski,
Gabriel. IV. Title: Human space flight. V. Title: U.S. human spaceflight.
TL789.8.U5H86 2007
629.450973--dc22

                                                                      2007022208

TABLE OF CONTENTS

PREFACE AND ACKNOWLEDGMENTS

This monograph is an updating of *U.S. Human Spaceflight: A Record of Achievement, 1961–1998* (Monograph in Aerospace History No. 9, July 1998), compiled by Judith A. Rumerman. It extends the timeframe covered through the end of calendar year 2006. It also includes additional information, such as more detailed crew and mission descriptions, more bibliographic information, Shuttle payload information, and useful Web sites. It also includes a new section on the International Space Station, which did not physically exist when the previous monograph was prepared and published. In addition, with Chris Gamble's guidance, Gabriel Okolski pulled together a new set of photos to illustrate this updated monograph.

For more information about NASA's human spaceflight efforts, please see *http://spaceflight.nasa.gov*, and for more about NASA history, please see *http://history.nasa.gov* online.

The captions for the images in this publication include NASA image numbers in parentheses. The numbers with GPN prefixes refer to images in the Great Images in NASA (GRIN) photo database, available at *http://grin.hq.nasa.gov* online.

Thanks to Kipp Teague for all his help with images for this publication and over the years in general. Thanks also to the production professionals who made this monograph possible. Specifically, thanks to Dyana Weis and Lisa Jirousek for copyediting it carefully, to graphic designer Steve Bradley for laying it out, to printing specialist Dave Dixon for handling this crucial final stage, and to Gail Carter-Kane and Cindy Miller for professionally overseeing all of these production phases.

We hope you enjoy this updated monograph and find it to be a useful reference work.

Stephen Garber
NASA History Division

INTRODUCTION

More than 45 years after the Mercury astronauts made their first brief forays into the new ocean of space, Earth orbit has become a busy arena of human activity. In that time, more than 300 people have traveled into orbit on U.S. spacecraft. The first astronauts went along stuffed into capsules barely large enough for their bodies, eating squeeze-tube food and peering out at Earth through tiny portholes. Their flights lasted only a matter of hours. Today, we routinely launch seven people at a time to spend a week living, working, and exploring aboard the Space Shuttle. In addition to regular launches, crew members from various nations keep a permanent human presence aboard the International Space Station (ISS).

The history of spaceflight has seen not only an increase in the numbers of people traveling into orbit, but also marked improvements in their vehicles. Each successive spacecraft, from Mercury through Apollo and the Space Shuttle, has been larger, more comfortable, and more capable. Scientists working inside the Shuttle's Spacelab have many of the comforts of a laboratory on Earth, none of which were available when human spaceflight first began.

Some projects, like Apollo, produced stunning firsts or explored new territory. Others—notably, Skylab and the Space Shuttle—advanced our capabilities by extending the range and sophistication of human operations in space. Both kinds of activity are vital to establishing a permanent human presence off Earth.

Almost 50 years after the dawn of the age of spaceflight, we are learning not just to travel into space, but also to live and stay there. That challenge ensures that the decades to come will be just as exciting as the past decades have been.

MERCURY

Overview

Project Mercury came into being on 7 October 1958, only a year and three days after the Soviet Union's *Sputnik I* satellite opened the Space Age. The goal of sending people into orbit and back had been discussed for many years before that, but with the initiation of the Mercury project, theory became engineering reality.

Mercury engineers had to devise a vehicle that would protect a human being from the temperature extremes, vacuum, and newly discovered radiation of space. Added to these demands was the need to keep an astronaut cool during the burning, high-speed reentry through the atmosphere. The vehicle that best fit these requirements was a wingless "capsule" designed for a ballistic reentry, with an ablative heatshield that burned off as Mercury returned to Earth.

Mercury capsules rode into space on two different kinds of boosters. The first suborbital flights were launched on Redstone rockets designed by Wernher von Braun's team in Huntsville, Alabama. For orbital flights, Mercury was placed on top of an Atlas-D, a modified ballistic missile whose steel skin was so thin (to save weight) it would have collapsed like a bag if not pressurized from within.

The first Americans to venture into space were drawn from a group of 110 military pilots chosen because they had flight-test experience and met certain physical requirements. Seven of those 110 became astronauts in April 1959. Six of the seven flew Mercury missions (Deke Slayton was removed from flight status due to a heart condition). Beginning with Alan Shepard's *Freedom 7* flight, the astronauts named their own spacecraft, and all added "7" to the name to acknowledge the teamwork of their fellow astronauts.

With only 12.133 cubic meters (428.47 cubic feet) of volume, the Mercury capsule was barely big enough to include its pilot. Inside were 120 controls, 55 electrical switches, 30 fuses, and 35 mechanical levers. Before Shepard's flight, surrogate "passengers" tested the integrity of the spacecraft design: two rhesus monkeys, Ham the chimpanzee, and an electronic "crewman simulator" mannequin that could breathe in and out to test the cabin environment. Finally, in May 1961, Shepard became the first American in space. Nine months later, John Glenn became the first American to orbit Earth.

The six Mercury flights (which totaled 2 days and 6 hours in space) taught the pioneers of spaceflight several important lessons. They learned not only that humans could function in space, but also that they were critical to a mission's success. Ground engineers learned the difficulty of launch preparations and found that a worldwide communications network was essential for human spaceflight.

By the time of the last Mercury flight in May 1963, the focus of the U.S. space program had already shifted. President John F. Kennedy had announced the goal of reaching the Moon only three weeks after Shepard's relatively simple 15-minute suborbital flight, and by 1963, only 500 of the 2,500 people working at NASA's Manned Spacecraft Center were still working on

Mercury Atlas 9 on the pad. (63C-1417)

Mercury program astronaut group portrait. Front row, left to right: Walter Schirra, Deke Slayton, John Glenn, and Scott Carpenter. Back row, left to right: Alan Shepard, Gus Grissom, and Gordon Cooper. (GPN-2000-000651)

Mercury—the remainder were already busy on Gemini and Apollo. But Mercury had taken the critical first step and had given reassuring answers to a number of fundamental questions:

Could humans survive in space?

Could a spacecraft be designed to launch them into orbit?

Could they return safely to Earth?

At the moment John Glenn's *Friendship 7* capsule was placed into its orbital trajectory, fulfilling the primary goal of Project Mercury, one member of the launch team on the ground made a notation in his log: "We are through the gates."

Mercury Statistics

Dates: 1961–1963

Vehicles: Redstone and Atlas launchers, Mercury spacecraft

Number of People Flown: 6

Highlights: First American in space, first American in orbit

Mercury Bibliography

NASA Sources

Grimwood, James M. *Project Mercury: A Chronology.* NASA SP-4001, 1963. Available online at *http://history.nasa.gov/SP-4001/cover.htm*.

Hansen, James R. *Spaceflight Revolution: NASA Langley Research Center from Sputnik to Apollo.* NASA SP-4308, 1995. Available online at *http://history.nasa.gov/SP-4308/sp4308.htm*.

Link, Mae Mills. *Space Medicine in Project Mercury.* NASA SP-4003, 1965. Available online at *http://history.nasa.gov/SP-4003/cover.htm*.

Pitts, John A. *The Human Factor: Biomedicine in the Manned Space Program to 1980.* NASA SP-4213, 1985. Available online at *http://history.nasa.gov/SP-4213/sp4213.htm*.

Swenson, Loyd S., Jr., James M. Grimwood, and Charles C. Alexander. *This New Ocean: A History of Project Mercury.* NASA SP-4201, 1966. Available online at *http://history.nasa.gov/SP-4201/cover.htm*.

Results of the Second U.S. Manned Orbital Space Flight. NASA SP-6, 1962. Available online at *http://history.nasa.gov/SP-6/cover.htm*.

Results of the Third U.S. Manned Orbital Space Flight. NASA SP-12, 1962. Available online at *http://history.nasa.gov/SP-12/cover.htm*.

Mercury Project Summary Including Results of the Fourth Manned Orbital Flight. NASA SP-45, 1963. Available online at *http://history.nasa.gov/SP-45/cover.htm*.

Non-NASA Sources

Catchpole, John. *Project Mercury: NASA's First Manned Space Programme.* Springer-Praxis, 2001.

Wolfe, Tom. *The Right Stuff.* Farrar, Straus & Giroux, 1979.

Mercury Astronauts. *We Seven.* Simon and Schuster, 1962.

Technicians working in the McDonnell White Room on the Mercury spacecraft. (GPN-2002-000040)

Liftoff of Mercury-Redstone 3. (GPN-2000-000859)

Alan Shepard waits to be sealed inside *Freedom 7.* (61-10515)

Mercury Missions

Mercury-Redstone 3 (*Freedom* 7)
5 May 1961
Crew: Alan B. Shepard, Jr.

Alan Shepard's suborbital flight lasted only 15 minutes, but it proved that an astronaut could survive and work comfortably in space and demonstrated to the 45 million Americans watching on TV that the United States was now in the spaceflight business. *Freedom* 7 was a ballistic "cannon shot"—Shepard reached no higher than 187.45 kilometers (116.5 statute miles) and traveled only 486.022 kilometers (302 statute miles) downrange from Cape Canaveral. During his short time in space, he maneuvered his spacecraft using hand controllers that pitched, yawed, and rolled the tiny Mercury capsule with small thrusters. He found the ride smoother than expected and reported no discomfort during 5 minutes of weightlessness. Although this first Mercury capsule lacked a window, Shepard was able to look down at the Atlantic coastline through a periscope. His view, though, was in black and white—the astronaut had inadvertently left a gray filter in place while waiting on the pad for liftoff.

Mercury-Redstone 4 (*Liberty Bell* 7)
21 July 1961
Crew: Virgil I. "Gus" Grissom

Gus Grissom's suborbital mission was essentially a repeat of Shepard's, again using the Redstone launcher instead of the more powerful Atlas. Grissom's Mercury capsule had a few minor improvements, including new, easier-to-use hand controllers; a window; and an explosive side hatch, which the astronauts had requested for easier escape in case of an emergency. Since Shepard's flight had been overly busy, Grissom's duties were deliberately reduced, and he spent more time observing Earth. The only significant failure came at the end of the 15-minute flight, after *Liberty Bell* 7 had parachuted into the Atlantic Ocean near the Bahamas. While Grissom waited inside the floating capsule to be picked up by helicopter rescue teams, the side hatch opened, filling the tiny spacecraft with seawater. *Liberty Bell* 7 sank, but a wet Grissom was safely recovered and the Mercury program was able to move on to orbital flights.

Mercury-Atlas 6 (*Friendship* 7)
20 February 1962
Crew: John H. Glenn, Jr.

John Glenn's orbital flight—an American first—lasted 4 hours and 55 minutes, during which he circled Earth three times and observed everything from a dust storm in Africa to Australian cities from an altitude of 260.71 kilometers (162 statute miles). Glenn was the first American to see a sunrise and sunset from space and was the first photographer in orbit, having taken along a 35-millimeter Minolta camera purchased from a Cocoa Beach, Florida, drugstore. The most nerve-wracking moments of the flight came before and during reentry, when a signal received on the ground (erroneously, as it turned out) indicated that the capsule's heatshield had come loose. At one point, Glenn thought his shield was burning up and breaking away. He ran out of fuel trying to stop the capsule's bucking motion as it descended through the atmosphere, but it splashed down safely, 64.37 kilometers (40 statute miles) short of his target (preflight calculations of the spacecraft's weight had not considered the loss of on-board "consumables"). Glenn returned to Earth a national hero, having achieved Project Mercury's primary goal of sending an astronaut into orbit.

The *Liberty Bell 7* spacecraft has just sunk below the water. A Marine helicopter has astronaut Gus Grissom in harness and is bringing him out of the water. (S61-02819)

Astronaut John Glenn is being inserted into the Mercury spacecraft *Friendship 7* for the Mercury-Atlas 6 mission on launch day. (87PC-0069)

Mercury-Atlas 7 (*Aurora* 7)
24 May 1962
Crew: M. Scott Carpenter

The focus of Scott Carpenter's 5-hour *Aurora* 7 mission was on science. The full flight plan included the first study of liquids in weightlessness, Earth photography, and an attempt (ultimately unsuccessful) to observe a flare fired from the ground. At dawn of the third and final orbit, Carpenter inadvertently bumped his hand against the inside wall of the cabin and solved a mystery from the previous flight. The resulting bright shower of particles outside the capsule—what John Glenn had called "fireflies"—turned out to be ice particles shaken loose from the capsule's exterior. Like Glenn, Carpenter circled Earth three times. Partly because he had been distracted watching the fireflies and partly because of his busy schedule, Carpenter overshot his planned reentry mark and splashed down 402.34 kilometers (250 statute miles) off target.

Mercury-Atlas 8 (*Sigma* 7)
3 October 1962
Crew: Walter M. Schirra, Jr.

Walter Schirra's was the first of two longer-duration Mercury missions. After Carpenter's flawed reentry, the emphasis returned to engineering rather than science (Schirra even named his spacecraft *Sigma* for the mathematical and engineering symbol meaning "summation"). The six-orbit mission lasted 9 hours and 13 minutes, much of which Schirra spent in what he called "chimp configuration," a free drift that tested the Mercury's autopilot system. Schirra also tried "steering" by the stars (he found this difficult), took photographs with a Hasselblad camera, exercised with a bungee cord device, saw lightning in the atmosphere, broadcast the first live message from an American spacecraft to radio and TV listeners below, and made the first splashdown in the Pacific Ocean. This was the highest flight of the Mercury program, with an apogee of 283.24 kilometers (176 statute miles), but Schirra later claimed to be unimpressed with space scenery as compared to the view from high-flying aircraft. "Same old deal, nothing new," he told debriefers after the flight.

Mercury-Atlas 9 (*Faith* 7)
15–16 May 1963
Crew: L. Gordon Cooper, Jr.

If Schirra's mission was an endurance test, the final Mercury flight was a marathon. Gordon Cooper circled Earth 22.5 times and released the first satellite from a spacecraft, a 152.4-millimeter (6-inch) sphere with a beacon for testing the astronaut's ability to track objects visually in space. Although a balloon for measuring atmospheric drag failed to deploy properly, Cooper finally completed another Mercury experiment when he was able to spot a powerful, 44,000-watt xenon lamp shining up from the ground. (He also claimed to be able to see individual houses from orbit and even to see smoke from chimneys in the Tibetan highlands.) During his 34 hours in space, Cooper slept, spoke a prayer into his tape recorder, and took the best photographs of the Mercury program, including pictures of Earth's limb and infrared weather photographs. His mission was deemed a "great success." It was so successful, in fact, that it allowed Mercury officials to cancel a planned seventh flight and move on to the two-man Gemini program.

John Glenn in flight on Mercury-Atlas 6. (62-MA6-168)

Navy divers install a stabilizing flotation collar around Gordon Cooper's Mercury space capsule shortly after splashdown. (S63-07717)

GEMINI

Overview

Gemini was not a purely pioneering program like Mercury, nor did it have the excitement of Apollo—but its success was critical to the achievement of President Kennedy's goal of reaching the Moon "by decade's end."

The program was announced to the public on 3 January 1962, after Apollo was already well under way. Gemini's primary purpose was to demonstrate space rendezvous and docking, which are techniques that would be used during Apollo, when the lunar lander would separate from the Command Module (CM) in orbit around the Moon and then meet up with it again after the astronauts left the lunar surface. Gemini also sought to extend astronauts' stays in space to two weeks, longer than even the Apollo missions would require.

It was during the Gemini program that spaceflight became routine. Ten piloted missions left the launchpads of Cape Canaveral, Florida, in less than 20 months, and the Manned Spacecraft Center (renamed the Johnson Space Center in 1973) outside Houston, Texas, took over the role of Mission Control. Ground operations became smooth and efficient, due in part to fleetingly short launch windows—the Gemini XI window opened for only 2 seconds—dictated by the need to rendezvous with targets already in orbit. Meanwhile, 16 new astronauts chalked up experience in space.

The Gemini spacecraft (originally called Mercury Mark II) was an improvement on Mercury in both size and capability. Gemini weighed more than 3,628.72 kilograms (7,983.20 pounds)—twice the weight of Mercury—but, ironically, seemed more cramped, having only 50 percent more cabin space for twice as many people. Ejection seats replaced Mercury's escape rocket, and more storage space was added for the longer Gemini flights. The long-duration missions also required fuel cells instead of batteries for generating electrical power.

Unlike Mercury, which had only been able to change its orientation in space, Gemini needed real maneuvering capability in order to rendezvous with another spacecraft. Gemini would have to move forward, backward, and sideways in its orbital path, and even change orbits. The complexity of rendezvous demanded two people on board and more piloting than had been possible with Mercury. It also required the first on-board computers to calculate complicated rendezvous maneuvers.

Gemini rode into orbit on a Titan II launch vehicle. The target for rendezvous operations was an unpiloted Agena upper stage, which was launched ahead of the Gemini. After meeting up in orbit, the nose of the Gemini capsule then fit into a docking collar on the Agena.

To avoid long delays between flights, Gemini spacecraft were made more serviceable, with subsystems that could be removed and replaced easily. An adapter module fitted to the rear of the capsule (and jettisoned before reentry) carried on-board oxygen, fuel, and other consumable supplies.

Gemini gave U.S. astronauts their first real experience with living and working in space. They had to learn to sleep and keep house on long flights in crowded quar-

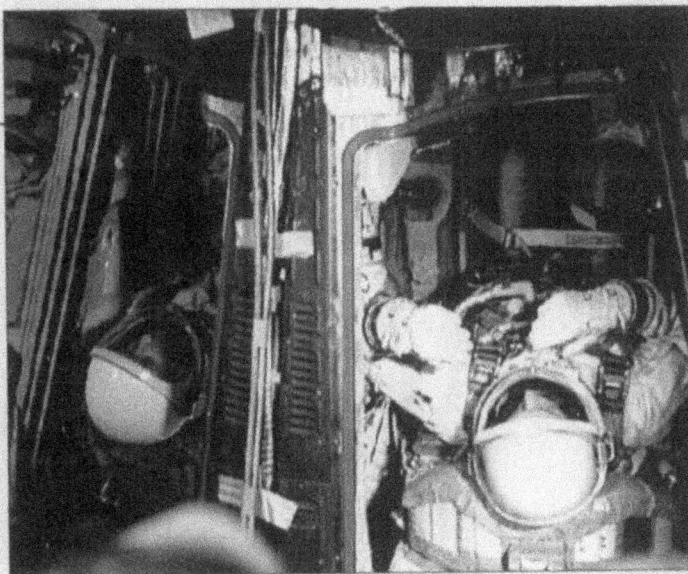

Astronauts James McDivitt and Ed White inside the Gemini spacecraft for a simulated launch at Cape Canaveral, Florida. (65P-0074)

The Gemini IX spacecraft was successfully launched from Kennedy Space Center on 3 June 1966. (S66-34098)

ters, both of which were difficult. Gemini astronauts also made the first forays outside their spacecraft, which required a new spacesuit design. Spacewalks proved more difficult than expected. Following Ed White's successful solo spacewalk on Gemini IV, it was not until the final Gemini flight that another extravehicular activity went as smoothly as planned.

By Gemini's end, an important new capability—orbital rendezvous and docking—had become routine, and doctors who had monitored the astronauts' health had gained confidence that humans could live, work, and stay healthy in space for days or even weeks at a time. Gemini also completed a long list of on-board science experiments, including studying the space environment and photographing Earth. Above all, the program added nearly 1,000 hours of valuable spaceflight experience in the years between Mercury and Apollo, which by 1966 was nearing flight readiness. Five days before the launch of the last Gemini, Lunar Orbiter 2 had been sent to the Moon, already scouting out Apollo landing sites.

Gemini Statistics

Dates: 1965–1966

Vehicles: Titan II launcher, Gemini spacecraft

Number of People Flown: 20

Highlights: First orbital rendezvous and docking, first U.S. spacewalk

Gemini Bibliography

NASA Sources

Dethloff, Henry C. *"Suddenly Tomorrow Came . . ."*: *A History of the Johnson Space Center*. NASA SP-4307, 1993. Available online at *http://www.jsc.nasa.gov/history/suddenly_tomorrow/suddenly.htm*.

Grimwood, James M., and Barton C. Hacker, with Peter J. Vorzimmer. *Project Gemini Technology and Operations: A Chronology*. NASA SP-4002, 1969. Available online at *http://history.nasa.gov/SP-4002/cover.htm*.

Hacker, Barton C., and James M. Grimwood. *On Shoulders of Titans: A History of Project Gemini*. NASA SP-4203, 1977. Available online at *http://history.nasa.gov/SP-4203/cover.htm*.

Pitts, John A. *The Human Factor: Biomedicine in the Manned Space Program to 1980*. NASA SP-4213, 1985. Available online at *http://history.nasa.gov/SP-4213/sp4213.htm*.

Non-NASA Sources

Collins, Michael. *Carrying the Fire: An Astronaut Journeys*. Farrar, Straus & Giroux, 1974.

Harland, David M. *How NASA Learned To Fly in Space: An Exciting Account of the Gemini Missions*. Apogee Books, 2004.

Shayler, David. Gemini: *Steps to the Moon*. Springer-Praxis, 2001.

During the Gemini missions, Mission Control shifted to Houston. (GPN-2000-001405)

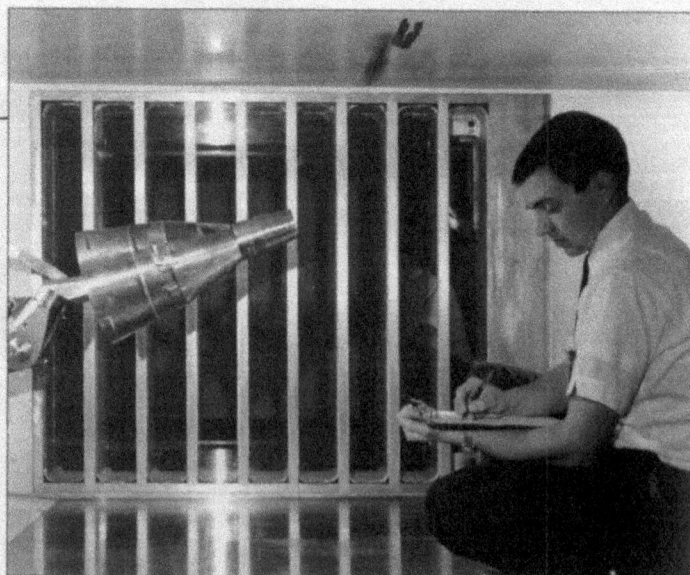
Gemini capsule being tested in Unitary Plan Wind Tunnel. (GPN-2000-001737)

Gemini Missions

Gemini III
23 March 1965
Crew: Virgil I. "Gus" Grissom and John W. Young

In a playful reference to the Broadway hit *The Unsinkable Molly Brown*, Gus Grissom nicknamed the Gemini III spacecraft *Molly Brown*, hoping that it would not duplicate his experience with *Liberty Bell 7*. (All Gemini flights were designated by a Roman numeral. Gemini III was the only flight to use both a Roman numeral and a call-sign/nickname given by an astronaut.) The mission's primary goal was to test the new, maneuverable Gemini spacecraft. In space, the crew fired thrusters to change the shape of their orbit, shift their orbital plane slightly, and drop to a lower altitude. The spacecraft was supposed to have enough lift for a precision landing, but reality did not match wind tunnel predictions: Gemini III splashed down some 111.1 kilometers (69 statute miles) short of its intended target. The capsule was designed to land on its side, suspended at two points from a parachute. But during the descent, when the astronauts threw a switch to shift *Molly Brown* to its landing position, they were thrown forward with such force that Grissom's faceplate cracked. Still, the first test of the two-seat spacecraft, and of Gemini ground operations, had been a success.

Gemini IV
3–7 June 1965
Crew: James A. McDivitt and Edward H. White II

The plan for this four-day, 62-orbit mission was for Gemini IV to fly in formation with the spent second stage of its Titan II booster in orbit. On this first attempt, however, spaceflight engineers learned something about the complication of orbital rendezvous. Thrusting toward their target, the astronauts only moved farther away. They finally gave up after using nearly half their fuel. (On later rendezvous missions, a spacecraft chasing another in orbit would first drop to a lower, faster orbit before rising again.) The mission's highlight was Edward White's 22-minute spacewalk, the first ever for an American. Tied to a tether and using a handheld "zip gun" to maneuver himself, White swam through space while James McDivitt took photographs. Gemini IV set a record for flight duration and eased fears about the medical consequences of longer missions. The new Mission Control Center outside Houston was put into use for the first time. It had to conduct the first three-shift operations because of the long flight duration.

Gemini V
21–29 August 1965
Crew: L. Gordon Cooper, Jr., and Charles "Pete" Conrad, Jr.

Gemini V doubled the spaceflight record to eight days, thanks to new fuel cells that generated enough electricity to power longer missions. Gordon Cooper and Pete Conrad were to have made a practice rendezvous with a "pod" deployed from the spacecraft, but problems with the electricity supply forced a switch to a simpler "phantom rendezvous," whereby the Gemini maneuvered to a predetermined position in space. Mercury veteran Cooper was the first person to travel into space twice. He and Conrad took high-resolution photographs for the Department of Defense (DOD), but problems with the fuel cells and maneuvering system forced the cancellation of several other experiments. The astronauts found themselves mark-

Ed White steps out during Gemini IV. (S65-30431)

Gus Grissom visible through the window of Gemini III before launch. (S65-24721)

ing time in orbit, and Conrad later lamented that he had not brought along a book. On-board medical tests, however, continued to show the feasibility of longer flights.

Gemini VII
4–18 December 1965
Crew: Frank Borman and James A. Lovell, Jr.

This 14-day mission required NASA to solve problems of long-duration spaceflight, not the least of which was stowage (the crew had practiced stuffing waste paper behind their seats before the flight). Timing their workday to match that of ground crews, both men worked and slept at the same time. Gemini VII flew the most experiments (20) of any Gemini mission, including studies of nutrition in space. The astronauts also evaluated a new, lightweight spacesuit, which proved uncomfortable if worn for a long time in Gemini's hot, cramped quarters. The high point of the mission was the rendezvous with Gemini VI. But the three days that followed were something of an endurance test, and both astronauts, heeding Pete Conrad's Gemini V advice, brought books along. Gemini VII was the longest spaceflight in U.S. history, until the Skylab missions of the 1970s.

Gemini VI-A
15–16 December 1965
Crew: Walter M. Schirra, Jr., and Thomas P. Stafford, Jr.

A rendezvous and docking with an unpiloted Agena target was this mission's original objective, but when Mission Control lost contact with the Agena during an October launch attempt, an alternate mission was substituted: a meeting in space of two Gemini spacecraft. Eight days after the launch of Borman and Lovell's Gemini VII, Walter Schirra and Thomas Stafford tried to join them, but their Titan II launcher shut down on the pad (the cool-headed Schirra did not eject, even though the countdown clock had started ticking—he felt no motion and trusted his senses). Three days later, Gemini VI made it into orbit. Using guidance from the computer as well as his own piloting, Schirra rendezvoused with the companion spacecraft in orbit on the afternoon of 15 December. Once in formation, the two Gemini capsules flew around each other, coming within 0.3048 meters (1 foot) of each other but never touching. The two spacecraft stayed in close proximity for 5 hours. One of Gemini's primary goals—orbital rendezvous—had been achieved.

Gemini VIII
16 March 1966
Crew: Neil A. Armstrong and David R. Scott

A second major objective of the Gemini program was completed less than 6 hours after launch, when Neil Armstrong brought Gemini VIII within 0.9144 meters (3 feet) of the prelaunched Agena target and slowly docked, completing the first orbital docking ever. What followed, however, were some of the most hair-raising minutes in space program history. The Gemini VIII capsule, still docked to the Agena, began rolling continuously. The crew undocked from the Agena, but the problem was a stuck thruster on the spacecraft that now tumbled even faster, at the dizzying rate of one revolution per second. The only way to stop the motion was to use the capsule's reentry control thrusters, which meant that Armstrong and David Scott had to cut short their mission and make an emergency return to Earth 10 hours after launch. They were still nauseated after splashdown, as well as disappointed: Scott had missed out on a planned spacewalk.

NASA attempted to launch Gemini VI at 9:54 a.m., 12 December 1965. However, seconds after ignition, the first-stage engine of the Gemini Launch Vehicle shut down due to the faulty release of a liftoff umbilical plug. (S65-59967)

This photograph of the Gemini VII spacecraft was taken from the hatch window of the Gemini VI spacecraft during rendezvous and station-keeping maneuvers at an altitude of approximately 160 miles on 15 December 1965. (S65-63197)

Gemini IX
3–6 June 1966
Crew: Thomas P. Stafford, Jr., and Eugene A. Cernan

Thomas Stafford and Eugene Cernan became the first multiperson backup crew to fly in space after the intended first crew of Elliott See and Charles Bassett died in a plane crash four months before the flight. The highlight of the mission was to have been a docking with a shortened Agena called the Augmented Target Docking Adapter (ATDA). The docking was canceled, though, after Stafford and Cernan rendezvoused with the target and found its protective shroud still attached, which made it look, in Stafford's words, like an "angry alligator." Cernan also was to have tested an Astronaut Maneuvering Unit (AMU), a jet-powered backpack stowed outside in Gemini's adapter module to which the spacewalking astronaut was to have strapped himself. But Cernan's spacewalk was troubled from the start. His visor fogged, he sweated and struggled with his tasks, and he had problems moving in microgravity. Everything took longer than expected, and Cernan had to go inside before getting a chance to fly the AMU. The device was not finally tested in space until Skylab, seven years later.

Gemini X
18–21 July 1966
Crew: John W. Young and Michael Collins

Gemini established that radiation at high attitude was not a problem. After docking with their Agena booster in low orbit, John Young and Michael Collins used it to climb another 482.8 kilometers (300 statute miles) to meet with the dead, drifting Agena left over from the

aborted Gemini VIII flight, thus executing the program's first double rendezvous. With no electricity on board the second Agena, the rendezvous was accomplished using only the astronauts' eyes for guides—no radar. After the rendezvous, Collins spacewalked over to the dormant Agena at the end of a 15.24-meter (50-foot) tether, making Collins the first person to meet another spacecraft in orbit. He retrieved a cosmic dust-collecting panel from the side of the Agena but returned no pictures of his close encounter—in the complicated business of keeping his tether clear of the Gemini and Agena, Collins's Hasselblad camera worked itself free and drifted off into orbit.

Gemini XI
12–15 September 1966
Crew: Charles "Pete" Conrad, Jr., and Richard F. Gordon, Jr.

With Apollo looming on the horizon, Gemini project managers wanted to accomplish a rendezvous immediately after reaching orbit, just as it would have to be done around the Moon. Only 85 minutes after launch, Pete Conrad and Richard Gordon matched orbits with their Agena target stage and docked several times. Conrad had originally hoped for a Gemini flight around the Moon but had to settle for the highest Earth orbit—1,367.94 kilometers (850 statute miles)—ever reached by an American manned spacecraft. Gordon's first spacewalk once again proved more difficult than ground simulations and had to be cut short when he became overtired. A second, 2-hour "stand-up" spacewalk went more smoothly. Gordon even fell asleep while floating halfway out the hatch. An experiment to link the Agena and Gemini vehicles with a 15.24-meter (50-foot) tether (which Gordon

The Agena Target Vehicle as seen from the Gemini VIII spacecraft during rendezvous. (S66-25781)

The Augmented Target Docking Adapter (ATDA) as seen from the Gemini IX spacecraft during one of their three rendezvous in space. Failure of the docking adapter protective cover to fully separate on the ATDA prevented the docking of the two spacecraft. The ATDA was described by the Gemini IX crew as an "angry alligator." (S66-37923)

had attached during his spacewalk) and rotate the joined pair was troublesome. Conrad had problems keeping the tether taut but was able to generate a modicum of "artificial gravity." The mission ended with the first totally automatic, computer-controlled reentry, which brought Gemini XI down only 4.5 kilometers (2.8 statute miles) from its recovery ship.

Gemini XII
11–15 November 1966
Crew: James A. Lovell, Jr., and Edwin E.
         "Buzz" Aldrin, Jr.

By the time of the last Gemini flight, the program still had not demonstrated that an astronaut could work easily and efficiently outside the spacecraft. In preparation for Gemini XII, new, improved restraints were added to the outside of the capsule, and a new technique—underwater training—was introduced, which would become a staple of all future spacewalk simulation. Buzz Aldrin's 2-hour-and-9-minute tethered spacewalk, during which he photographed star fields, retrieved a micrometeorite collector, and did other chores, at last demonstrated the feasibility of extravehicular activity. Two more stand-up spacewalks also went smoothly, as did the by now routine rendezvous and docking with an Agena, which was done "manually" using the on-board computer and charts when a rendezvous radar failed. The climb to a higher orbit, however, was canceled because of a problem with the Agena booster.

Gemini VII, viewed from Gemini VI. (S65-63189)

Atlas Agena target vehicle liftoff for Gemini XI from Pad 14. (GPN-2000-001019)

APOLLO

Overview

The Apollo program had been under way since July 1960, when NASA announced a follow-on to Mercury that would fly astronauts around the Moon. But with President John F. Kennedy's speech on 25 May 1961 declaring the goal of landing an astronaut on the surface of the Moon and returning to Earth by decade's end, Apollo shifted its focus. That goal was achieved with five months to spare when on 20 July 1969, Neil Armstrong and Edwin "Buzz" Aldrin touched down in the Sea of Tranquility.

Apollo was one of the great triumphs of modern technology. Six expeditions landed on the Moon, and one, Apollo 13, was forced to return without landing. Before that, there had been two crewed checkouts of Apollo hardware in Earth orbit and two lunar orbit missions.

The Apollo Lunar Module was the first true spacecraft designed to fly only in a vacuum, with no aerodynamic qualities whatsoever. Launched attached to the Apollo Command and Service Module (CSM), it separated in lunar orbit and descended to the Moon with two astronauts inside. At the end of its stay on the surface, the Lunar Module's ascent stage fired its own rocket to rejoin the Command/Service Module in lunar orbit.

The teardrop-shaped Apollo Command Module (CM), the living quarters for the three-person crews, had a different shape than that of the conical-nosed Gemini and Mercury. The attached cylindrical Service Module contained supplies as well as the Service Propulsion System engine that placed the vehicle in and out of lunar orbit.

Boosting the Apollo vehicles to the Moon was the job of the giant Saturn V—the first launch vehicle large enough that it had to be assembled away from the launchpad and transported there. A fueled Saturn V weighed more than 2.7 million kilograms (2,970 tons) at liftoff and stood 110.64 meters (362.9 feet) high with the Apollo vehicle on top. The vehicle had three stages—the S-IC, S-II, and S-IVB—the last of which burned to send Apollo out of Earth orbit and on its way to the Moon.

The Apollo program greatly increased the pace and complexity of ground operations, both before launch and during the missions, when ground controllers had to track two spacecraft at the same time. The lunar missions also required extensive training. Apollo astronauts logged some 84,000 hours—their combined time equaled nearly 10 years—practicing for their flights, including everything from simulations of lunar gravity to geology field trips to flying the lunar lander training vehicle.

On 27 January 1967, just as the program was nearing readiness for its first manned flight, tragedy struck. A fire inside an Apollo Command Module took the lives of astronauts Virgil "Gus" Grissom, Edward White, and Roger Chaffee, who were training inside it at the time. The fire resulted in delays and modifications to the spacecraft, but by October 1968, Apollo 7 was ready to carry three astronauts into Earth orbit. There, they checked out the Command and Service Module (which had been tested in an unpiloted mode during the November 1967 Apollo 4 mission, which was also the first flight of the Saturn V). By December 1968, Apollo 8 was ready to try for lunar orbit (on the Saturn V's third outing), and seven months later, Apollo 11 made the first lunar landing.

The Saturn V first stages, S-1C-10, S-1C-11, and S-1C-9, are in the horizontal assembly area for the engine (five F-1 engines) installation at Michoud Assembly Facility. (GPN-2000-000048)

A technician works atop the white room through which the Apollo 11 astronauts will enter their spacecraft. The vehicle is being prepared for the first piloted lunar landing mission. (GPN-2000-000625)

By the time the Apollo program ended in 1972, astronauts had extended the range and scope of their lunar explorations. The final three lunar missions were far more sophisticated than the first three, in large part because the astronauts carried a lunar rover that allowed them to roam miles from their base. Apollo 11's Neil Armstrong and Buzz Aldrin spent only 2.5 hours walking on the Moon's surface. On Apollo 17, the moonwalks totaled 22 hours and the astronauts spent three days "camped out" in the Moon's Taurus-Littrow valley.

After six lunar landings, the Apollo program came to a conclusion (the Apollo 18, 19, and 20 missions had been canceled in 1970 because of budget limitations), and with it ended the first wave of human exploration of the Moon.

Apollo Statistics

Dates: 1967–1972

Vehicles: Saturn IB and Saturn V launch vehicles, Apollo Command and Service Module, Lunar Module

Number of People Flown: 33

Highlights: First humans to leave Earth orbit, first human landing on the Moon

Apollo Bibliography

NASA Sources

Benson, Charles D., and William Barnaby Faherty. *Moonport: A History of Apollo Launch Facilities and Operations*. NASA SP-4204, 1978. Available online at *http://history.nasa.gov/SP-4204/cover.html*.

Bilstein, Roger E. *Stages to Saturn: A Technological History of the Apollo/Saturn Launch Vehicles*. NASA SP-4206, 1980. Available online at *http://history.nasa.gov/SP-4206/sp4206.htm*.

Brooks, Courtney G., and Ivan D. Ertel. *The Apollo Spacecraft: A Chronology, Volume III: October 1, 1964–January 20, 1966*. NASA SP-4009, 1973. Available online at *http://history.nasa.gov/SP-4009/cover.htm*.

Brooks, Courtney G., James M. Grimwood, and Loyd S. Swenson, Jr. *Chariots for Apollo: A History of Manned Lunar Spacecraft*. NASA SP-4205, 1979. Available online at *http://history.nasa.gov/SP-4205/cover.html*.

Compton, W. David. *Where No Man Has Gone Before: A History of Apollo Lunar Exploration Missions*. NASA SP-4214, 1989. Available online at *http://history.nasa.gov/SP-4214/cover.html*.

Cortright, Edgar. *Apollo Expeditions to the Moon*. NASA SP-350, 1975. Available online at *http://history.nasa.gov/SP-350/cover.html*.

Dethloff, Henry C. *"Suddenly Tomorrow Came . . .": A History of the Johnson Space Center*. NASA SP-4307, 1993. Available online at *http://www.jsc.nasa.gov/history/suddenly_tomorrow/suddenly.htm*.

Ertel, Ivan D., and Mary Louise Morse. *The Apollo Spacecraft: A Chronology, Volume I*. NASA SP-4009, 1969. Available online at *http://history.nasa.gov/SP-4009/cover.htm*.

Ertel, Ivan D., and Roland W. Newkirk, with Courtney G. Brooks. *The Apollo Spacecraft: A Chronology, Volume IV: January 21, 1966–July 13, 1974*. NASA SP-4009, 1978. Available online at *http://history.nasa.gov/SP-4009/cover.htm*.

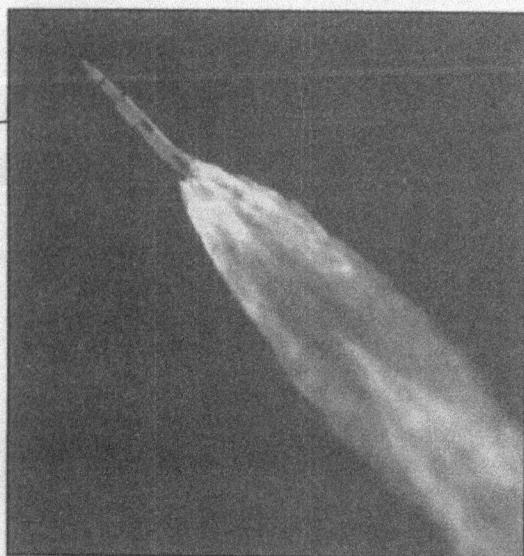

The Apollo 10 space vehicle is launched from Pad B, Launch Complex 39, Kennedy Space Center, on 18 May 1969. (S69-34481)

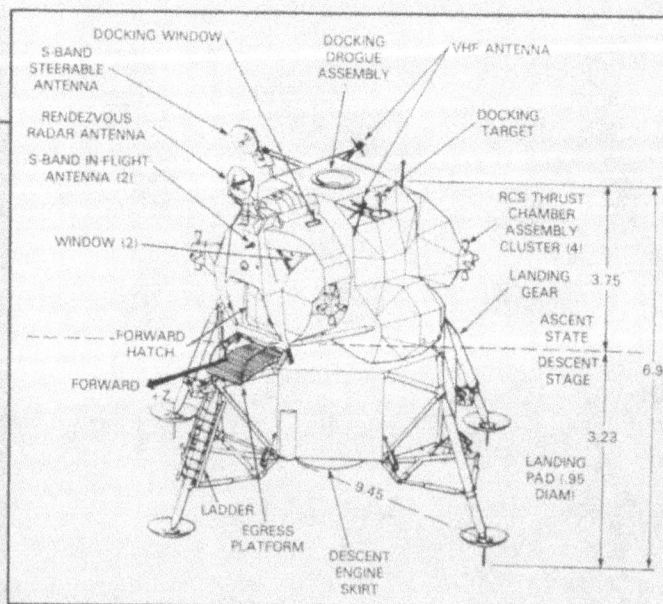

Diagram of the Lunar Module. (*http://history.nasa.gov/diagrams/apollo.html*)

Fries, Sylvia D. *NASA Engineers and the Age of Apollo.* NASA SP-4104, 1992. Available online at *http://history. nasa.gov/SP-4104/sp4104.htm.*

Hansen, James R. *Spaceflight Revolution: NASA Langley Research Center from Sputnik to Apollo.* NASA SP-4308, 1995. Available online at *http://history.nasa.gov/SP-4308/ sp4308.htm.*

Herring, Mack R. *Way Station to Space: A History of the John C. Stennis Space Center.* NASA SP-4310, 1997. Available online at *http://history.nasa.gov/SP-4310/sp4310.htm.*

Levine, Arnold S. *Managing NASA in the Apollo Era.* NASA SP-4102, 1982. Available online at *http://history. nasa.gov/SP-4102/sp4102.htm.*

Morse, Mary Louise, and Jean Kernahan Bays. *The Apollo Spacecraft: A Chronology, Volume II: November 8, 1962–September 30, 1964.* NASA SP-4009, 1973. Available online at *http:// history.nasa.gov/SP-4009/cover.htm.*

Pitts, John A. *The Human Factor: Biomedicine in the Manned Space Program to 1980.* NASA SP-4213, 1985. Available online at *http://history.nasa.gov/SP-4213/sp4213.htm.*

Non-NASA Sources

Armstrong, Neil A., Michael Collins, and Edwin E. Aldrin. *First on the Moon.* Little, Brown and Company, 1970.

Chaikin, Andrew. *A Man on the Moon.* Viking, 1994.

Cooper, Henry S. F. *Apollo on the Moon.* Dial Press, 1969.

———. *Moon Rocks.* Dial Press, 1970.

———. *Thirteen: The Flight that Failed.* Dial Press, 1973.

Harland, David M. *The First Men on the Moon: The Story of Apollo 11.* Springer-Praxis, 2006.

Lambright, W. Henry. *Powering Apollo: James E. Webb of NASA.* Johns Hopkins University Press, 1995.

Lewis, Richard S. *The Voyages of Apollo: The Exploration of the Moon.* Quadrangle, 1974.

Logsdon, John M. *The Decision to Go to the Moon: Project Apollo and the National Interest.* The MIT Press, 1970.

McDougall, Walter A. . . . *The Heavens and the Earth: A Political History of the Space Age.* Johns Hopkins University Press, rep. ed. 1997.

Murray, Charles A., and Catherine Bly Cox. *Apollo: The Race to the Moon.* Simon and Schuster, 1989.

Orloff, Richard W., and David M. Harland. *Apollo: The Definitive Sourcebook.* Springer-Praxis, 2006.

Pellegrino, Charles R., and Joshua Stoff. *Chariots for Apollo: The Making of the Lunar Module.* Atheneum, 1985.

Wilhelms, Don E. *To a Rocky Moon: A Geologist's History of Lunar Exploration.* University of Arizona Press, 1993.

Web Sites

NASA History Division Apollo Web site: *http://history. nasa.gov/apollo.html*

The Apollo Surface Journal: *http://history.nasa.gov/alsj/*

Kipp Teague's Apollo Web site: *http://www.apolloarchive.com/*

View of docked Apollo 9 Command and Service Module and Lunar Module as David Scott egresses. (AS09-20-3064)

Apollo 9 Lunar Module in lunar landing configuration. (AS09-21-3199)

Apollo Missions

Apollo 7
11–22 October 1968
Crew: Walter M. Schirra, Jr., Donn F. Eisele,
       Walter Cunningham

Apollo 7 was a confidence builder. After the January 1967 Apollo launchpad fire, the Apollo Command Module had been extensively redesigned. Walter Schirra, the only astronaut to fly Mercury, Gemini, and Apollo missions, commanded this Earth-orbital shakedown of the Command and Service Modules. With no lunar lander, Apollo 7 could use the Saturn IB booster rather than the giant Saturn V. The Apollo hardware and all mission operations worked without any significant problems, and the Service Propulsion System (SPS), the all-important engine that would place Apollo in and out of lunar orbit, made eight nearly perfect firings. Even though Apollo's larger cabin was more comfortable than Gemini's, 11 days in orbit took its toll on the astronauts. The food was bad, and all three astronauts developed colds. But their mission proved the spaceworthiness of the basic Apollo vehicle.

Apollo 8
21–27 December 1968
Crew: Frank Borman, James A. Lovell, Jr.,
       William A. Anders

The Apollo 8 astronauts were the first human beings to venture beyond low-Earth orbit and visit another world. What was originally to have been an Earth-orbit checkout of the lunar lander became instead a race with the Soviets to become the first nation to orbit the Moon. The Apollo 8 crew rode inside the Command Module with no lunar lander attached. They were the first astronauts to be launched by the Saturn V, which had flown only twice before. The booster worked perfectly, as did the Service Propulsion System engines that had been checked out on Apollo 7. Apollo 8 entered lunar orbit on the morning of 24 December 1968. For the next 20 hours, the astronauts circled the Moon, which appeared out their windows as a gray, battered wasteland. They took photographs, scouted future landing sites, and on Christmas Eve read from the Book of Genesis to TV viewers back on Earth. They also photographed the first Earthrise as seen from the Moon. Apollo 8 proved the ability to navigate to and from the Moon and gave a tremendous boost to the entire Apollo program.

Apollo 9
3–13 March 1969
Crew: James A. McDivitt, David R. Scott, Russell L.
       "Rusty" Schweickart

Apollo 9 was the first space test of the third critical piece of Apollo hardware—the Lunar Module (LM). For 10 days, the astronauts put all three Apollo vehicles through their paces in Earth orbit, undocking and then redocking the lunar lander with the Command Module (CM), just as they would in lunar orbit. For this and all subsequent Apollo flights, the crews were allowed to name their own spacecraft. The gangly Lunar Module was *Spider*, and the CM was *Gumdrop*. Rusty Schweickart and David Scott performed a spacewalk, and Schweickart checked out the new Apollo spacesuit, the first to have its own life-support system rather than being dependent on an umbilical connection to the spacecraft. Apollo 9 gave proof that the Apollo machines were up to the task of orbital rendezvous and docking.

The prime crew of the first piloted Apollo space mission, from left to right, are Command Module pilot Donn Eisele, commander Walter Schirra, Jr., and Lunar Module pilot Walter Cunningham. (GPN-2000-001160)

The Transporter nears the top of the 5-percent incline at Launch Complex 39A with the Apollo 11 Saturn V. (69P-0410)

Apollo 10
18–26 May 1969
Crew: Thomas P. Stafford, Jr., John W. Young, Eugene A. Cernan

This dress rehearsal for a Moon landing brought Thomas Stafford and Eugene Cernan's Lunar Module named *Snoopy,* to within 9 miles of the lunar surface. Except for the final stretch, the mission went exactly as a landing would have gone both in space and on the ground, where Apollo's extensive tracking and control network was put through a dry run. Shortly after leaving low-Earth orbit, the Lunar Module and the Command and Service Module separated then redocked top to top. Upon reaching lunar orbit, they separated again. While John Young orbited the Moon alone in his Command Module, *Charlie Brown,* Stafford and Cernan checked out the Lunar Module's radar and ascent engine, rode out a momentary gyration in the lunar lander's motion (due to a faulty switch setting), and surveyed the Apollo 11 landing site in the Sea of Tranquility. This test article of the Lunar Module was not equipped to land, however. Apollo 10 also added another first—broadcasting live color TV from space.

Apollo 11
16–24 July 1969
Crew: Neil A. Armstrong, Michael Collins, Edwin E. "Buzz" Aldrin, Jr.

Half of Apollo's primary goal—a safe return—was achieved at 4:17 p.m. Eastern Daylight Time (EDT) on 20 July 1969 when Neil Armstrong piloted the *Eagle* to a touchdown on the Moon, with less than 30 seconds'

worth of fuel left in the Lunar Module. Six hours later, Armstrong took his famous "one giant leap for mankind." Buzz Aldrin joined him, and the two spent 2.5 hours drilling core samples, photographing what they saw, and collecting rocks. After more than 21 hours on the lunar surface, they returned to Michael Collins on board *Columbia,* bringing 20.87 kilograms (45.91 pounds) of lunar samples with them. The two moonwalkers had left behind scientific instruments, an American flag, and other mementos, including a plaque bearing the inscription: "Here Men From Planet Earth First Set Foot Upon the Moon. July 1969 A.D. We Came in Peace For All Mankind."

Apollo 12
14–24 November 1969
Crew: Charles "Pete" Conrad, Jr., Richard F. Gordon, Jr., Alan L. Bean

The second lunar landing was an exercise in precision targeting. The descent was automatic, with only a few manual corrections by Pete Conrad. The landing in the Ocean of Storms brought the Lunar Module *Intrepid* within walking distance (182.88 meters [600 feet]) of a robotic spacecraft that had touched down there two-and-a-half years earlier. Conrad and Alan Bean brought pieces of the Surveyor 3 back to Earth for analysis and took two moonwalks that lasted just under 4 hours each. They collected rocks and set up experiments that measured the Moon's seismicity, solar wind flux, and magnetic field. Meanwhile, Richard Gordon, aboard the *Yankee Clipper* in lunar orbit, took multispectral photographs of the surface. The crew stayed an extra day in lunar orbit taking photographs. When *Intrepid*'s ascent stage was dropped onto the Moon

The Apollo 11 crew conducts a crew compartment fit and functional check of the equipment and storage locations in their Command Module. Peering from the hatch are, from left to right, Neil Armstrong, commander; Michael Collins, Command Module pilot; and Buzz Aldrin, Lunar Module pilot. (69-H-957)

Buzz Aldrin, Lunar Module pilot, is photographed walking near the Lunar Module during the Apollo 11 extravehicular activity. Photographed by Neil Armstrong. (AS11-40-5903)

after Conrad and Bean rejoined Gordon in orbit, the seismometers the astronauts had left on the lunar surface registered the vibrations for more than an hour.

Apollo 13
11–17 April 1970
Crew: James A. Lovell, Jr., Fred W. Haise, Jr., John L. "Jack" Swigert, Jr.

The crew's understated radio message to Mission Control was "Okay, Houston, we've had a problem here." Within 321,860 kilometers (199,553.2 statute miles) of Earth, an oxygen tank in the Service Module exploded. The only solution was for the crew to abort their planned landing, swing around the Moon, and return on a trajectory back to Earth. Since their Command Module *Odyssey* was almost completely dead, the three astronauts had to use the Lunar Module *Aquarius* as a crowded lifeboat for the return home. The four-day return trip was cold, uncomfortable, and tense. But Apollo 13 proved the program's ability to weather a major crisis and bring the crew back home safely.

Apollo 14
31 January–9 February 1971
Crew: Alan B. Shepard, Jr., Stuart A. Roosa, Edgar D. Mitchell

After landing the Lunar Module *Antares* in the Fra Mauro region—the original destination for Apollo 13—Alan Shepard and Edgar Mitchell took two moonwalks, adding new seismic studies to the by now familiar Apollo experiment package and using a "lunar rickshaw" pullcart

to carry their equipment. A planned rock-collecting trip to the 304.8-meter-wide (1,000-foot-wide) Cone Crater was dropped, however, when the astronauts had trouble finding their way around the lunar surface. Although later estimates showed that they had made it to within 30.48 meters (100 feet) of the crater's rim, the explorers had become disoriented in the alien landscape. Stuart Roosa, meanwhile, took pictures from on board Command Module *Kitty Hawk* in lunar orbit. On the way back to Earth, the crew conducted the first U.S. materials processing experiments in space. The Apollo 14 astronauts were the last lunar explorers to be quarantined upon their return from the Moon.

Apollo 15
26 July–7 August 1971
Crew: David R. Scott, James B. Irwin, Alfred M. Worden

The first of the longer, expedition-style lunar landing missions was also the first to include the lunar rover, a car-like vehicle that extended the astronauts' range. The Lunar Module *Falcon* touched down near the sinuous channel known as Hadley Rille. David Scott and James Irwin rode more than 27 kilometers (16.74 statute miles) in their rover and had a free hand in their geological field studies compared to earlier lunar astronauts. They brought back one of the prize trophies of the Apollo program—a sample of ancient lunar crust nicknamed the "Genesis Rock." Apollo 15 also launched a small subsatellite for measuring particles and fields in the lunar vicinity. On the way back to Earth, Alfred Worden, who had flown solo on board *Endeavour* while his crewmates walked on the

Astronaut Alan Bean holds a Special Environmental Sample Container during an EVA on the Apollo 12 mission. (AS12-49-7278)

A sweeping view showing astronaut Alan Shepard, mission commander, and the Apollo 14 Lunar Module. (AS14-68-9487)

surface, conducted the first spacewalk between Earth and the Moon to retrieve film from the side of the spacecraft.

Apollo 16
16–27 April 1972
Crew: John W. Young, Thomas K. Mattingly II,
Charles M. Duke, Jr.

A malfunction in the main propulsion system of the Lunar Module *Orion* nearly caused their Moon landing to be scrubbed, but John Young and Charles Duke ultimately spent three days exploring the Descartes highland region, while Thomas Mattingly circled overhead in *Casper*. What was thought to have been a region of volcanism turned out not to be, based on the astronauts' discoveries. Their collection of returned specimens included an 11.34-kilogram (24.95-pound) chunk that was the largest single rock returned by the Apollo astronauts. The Apollo 16 astronauts also conducted performance tests with the lunar rover, at one time getting up to a top speed of 17.7 kilometers per hour (10.94 miles per hour).

Apollo 17
7–19 December 1972
Crew: Eugene A. Cernan, Ronald E. Evans,
Harrison H. "Jack" Schmitt

The last man to set foot on the Moon was also the first scientist—astronaut/geologist Jack Schmitt. While Ronald Evans circled in *America*, Schmitt and Eugene Cernan collected a record 108.86 kilograms (239.49 pounds) of rocks during three moonwalks. The crew roamed for 33.8 kilometers (20.96 statute miles) through the Taurus-Littrow valley in their rover, discovered orange-colored soil, and left behind a plaque attached to their lander *Challenger*, which read: "Here Man completed his first exploration of the Moon, December 1972 A.D. May the spirit of peace in which we came be reflected in the lives of all mankind." The Apollo lunar program had ended.

Charles Duke explores the Plum Crater during Apollo 16. (AS16-114-18423)

Astronaut David Scott, commander of Apollo 15, works at the Lunar Roving Vehicle (LRV) during the third lunar surface EVA of the mission at the Hadley-Apennine landing site. (AS15-82-11121)

Apollo 17 glides to a safe landing in the Pacific Ocean. (72-H-1550)

SKYLAB

Overview

NASA had studied concepts for space stations, including an inflatable, donut-shaped station, since the earliest days of the space program. But it was not until the Saturn rocket came into existence in the mid-1960s that the Skylab program was born. Initially called the Apollo Applications Program, Skylab was designed to use leftover Apollo hardware to achieve extended stays by astronauts in Earth orbit.

At first there were two competing concepts. The first was the so-called "wet" workshop, where a Saturn IB rocket would be launched and fueled and its S-IVB upper stage vented and refurbished in orbit. The second was the "dry" workshop, in which the outfitting of an empty S-IVB stage would be done on the ground beforehand and launched on a Saturn V. In July 1969, while the Apollo 11 astronauts were completing their historic lunar landing mission, program managers made their decision: the "dry" workshop concept won.

The *Skylab* space station weighed approximately 907,108 kilograms (100 tons). It was placed into orbit by the last Saturn V launch vehicle. Three separate astronaut crews then met up with the orbiting workshop using modified Apollo Command and Service Modules (CSM) launched by smaller Saturn IB rockets.

Skylab had a habitable volume of just over 283.17 cubic meters (10,000 cubic feet). It was divided into two levels separated by a metal floor, which was actually an open grid into which the astronauts' cleated shoes could be locked. The "upper" floor had storage lockers; a large,

empty volume for conducting experiments; plus two scientific airlocks, one pointing down at Earth, the other toward the Sun. The lower floor had compartmented "rooms" with many of the comforts of home: a dining room table, three bedrooms, a work area, a shower, and a bathroom.

The largest piece of scientific equipment, attached to one end of the cylindrical workshop, was the Apollo Telescope Mount (ATM), used to study the Sun in different wavelengths with no atmospheric interference. The ATM had its own electricity-generating solar panels. *Skylab* also had an airlock module for spacewalks (required for repairs, experiment deployments, and routine changing of film in the ATM). The Apollo Command and Service Module remained attached to the station's multiple docking adapter while the astronauts were on board.

The space station itself was launched 14 May 1973, on the unpiloted Skylab 1 mission. Beginning only 63 seconds after the launch, however, the workshop's combination meteorite shield and sunshade was torn loose by aerodynamic stress, taking one of the two electricity-producing solar arrays with it and preventing the other from deploying properly. The crew was supposed to have launched the next day, but they waited on the ground for 10 days while a fix was worked out (see Skylab 2).

In the course of the next nine months, three different crews lived aboard *Skylab* for one, two, then three months at a time. The station, which orbited at an altitude of 434.52 kilometers (269.4 statute miles), was deactivated between flights. Together, the nine *Skylab* astronauts chalked up a combined total of 513 days in orbit, during which they conducted thousands of experi-

Skylab shroud installed in NASA Lewis Research Center's (now known as Glenn Research Center) Plum Brook Station Space Power Facility. The shroud protected the upper section of the *Skylab* space station, including its solar power arrays. (GPN-2000-001462)

On 23 May 1973, Dr. James Fletcher, Administrator for NASA, appeared before the United States Senate Committee on Aeronautical and Space Sciences. Dr. Fletcher explained to the committee what methods would be attempted to repair the damaged *Skylab*. He stated that if the planned repairs were successful, it would be possible to accomplish most of the activities scheduled for the two subsequent Skylab missions, each lasting 56 days. (GPN-2000-001627)

ments and observations, studying (in decreasing order of the amount of crew time spent) solar astronomy, life sciences, Earth observations, astrophysics, human/systems studies, Comet Kohoutek observations (Skylab 4 only), materials science, and student experiments.

Skylab showed the value of having humans working for long periods in orbit on a wide variety of scientific studies and proved that they could survive the ordeal. The empty *Skylab* station reentered and burned up in the atmosphere on 11 July 1979, more than five years after the last crew left.

Skylab Statistics

Dates: 1973–1974

Vehicles: Skylab orbital workshop (launched on a Saturn V rocket), Saturn IB launch vehicle (for crews)

Number of People Flown: 9

Highlights: Longest-duration spaceflights in U.S. history

Bibliography

NASA Sources

Compton, W. David, and Charles D. Benson. *Living and Working in Space: A History of Skylab.* NASA SP-4208, 1983. Available online at *http://history.nasa.gov/SP-4208/sp4208.htm.*

Newkirk, Roland W., and Ivan D. Ertel, with Courtney G. Brooks. *Skylab:A Chronology.* NASA SP-4011, 1977. Available online at *http://history.nasa.gov/SP-4011/cover.htm.*

Pitts, John A. *The Human Factor: Biomedicine in the Manned Space Program to 1980.* NASA SP-4213, 1985. Available online at *http://history.nasa.gov/SP-4213/sp4213.htm.*

Non-NASA Sources

Shayler, David. *Skylab: America's Space Station.* Springer-Praxis, 2001.

Skylab 2
25 May–22 June 1973
Crew: Charles "Pete" Conrad, Jr., Paul J. Weitz, Joseph P. Kerwin

The first crew to visit the *Skylab* space station started its mission with home repairs. *Skylab*'s combination meteorite shield and sunshield had torn loose during launch and one of its two remaining solar panels was jammed. Because of concerns that high temperatures inside the workshop—the result of having no sunshield—would release toxic materials and ruin on-board film and food, the crew had to work fast. After a failed attempt to deploy the stuck solar panel, they set up a "parasol" as a replacement sunshade. The fix worked, and temperatures inside dropped low enough that the crew could enter. Two weeks later, Pete Conrad and Joseph Kerwin conducted a spacewalk and, after a struggle, were able to free the stuck solar panel and begin the flow of electricity to their new "home." For nearly a month they made further repairs to the workshop, conducted medical experiments, gathered solar and Earth science data, and returned some 29,000 frames of film. The Skylab 2 astronauts spent 28 days in space, a time that doubled the previous U.S. record.

Two seamstresses stitch together a sunshade for the Skylab Orbital Workshop, the first U.S. experimental space station in orbit, which lost its thermal protection shield during the launch on 14 May 1973. (7040525)

Gerald Carr balances William Pogue on his finger. (SL4-150-5080)

Skylab 3
28 July–25 September 1973
Crew: Alan L. Bean, Jack R. Lousma, Owen K. Garriott

After an early bout of motion sickness, the three-person Skylab 3 crew settled down to a 59-day stay aboard the space station. During the flight, Owen Garriott and Jack Lousma deployed a second sunshield on a spacewalk lasting 6.5 hours, the first and longest of three Skylab 3 spacewalks. During their two months in orbit, the astronauts continued a busy schedule of experiments, including a student experiment to determine whether spiders could spin webs in weightlessness (they could). They also tested a jet-powered Astronaut Maneuvering Unit (AMU) backpack inside the spacious volume of Skylab's forward compartment, which had been carried but never flown on Gemini missions in the 1960s. The AMU proved a capable form of one-man space transportation and helped engineers design the more sophisticated Manned Maneuvering Unit (MMU) used on the Space Shuttle in the 1980s.

Skylab 4
16 November 1973–8 February 1974
Crew: Gerald P. Carr, William R. Pogue, Edward G. Gibson

Clocking in at 84 days, 1 hour, 15 minutes, and 31 seconds, Skylab 4 remains the longest U.S. spaceflight to date. To help keep the crew in shape, a treadmill was added to the on-board bicycle-like ergometer. As a result of the exercise, the Skylab 4 crew was in better physical condition upon their return to Earth than previous Skylab crews, even though an excessive work pace had caused some tension during the flight. Comet Kohoutek was among the special targets observed by the Skylab 4 crew, as were a solar eclipse and solar flares. The astronauts conducted four spacewalks, including one on Christmas Day to view Kohoutek, and set records for time spent on experiments in every discipline from medical investigations to materials science.

Scientist-astronaut Owen Garriott, Skylab 3 science pilot, is seen performing an extravehicular activity at the Apollo Telescope Mount (ATM) of the Skylab space station cluster in Earth orbit. (GPN-2002-000065)

The crew members of Skylab 3: foreground, astronaut Alan Bean, commander; left, scientist-astronaut Owen Garriott, science pilot; and astronaut Jack Lousma, pilot. (72-HC-90)

View of the Skylab Orbital Workshop in Earth orbit from the Command and Service Module. (SL4-143-4706)

APOLLO-SOYUZ

Overview

The final mission of the Apollo era, in July 1975, was the first in which spacecraft from two nations rendezvoused and docked in orbit. The idea for this U.S./Soviet "handshake in space" had been initiated three years earlier with an agreement signed by U.S. President Richard Nixon and Soviet President Aleksey Kosygin.

The American crew for this goodwill flight included Thomas Stafford, a veteran of three flights, Vance Brand, who had never flown in space, and Mercury astronaut Deke Slayton, the only one of the original seven astronauts who had never flown (due to a heart condition). The American astronauts traveled into orbit inside a three-person Apollo spacecraft.

Similar in function to the Apollo Command Module, the two-person *Soyuz* capsule flown by the Soviets had debuted in 1967. Aboard the Soviet spacecraft were Alexei Leonov, who had made history's first spacewalk in 1965, and rookie Valery Kubasov.

The Apollo-*Soyuz* mission, aside from its political significance, resulted in a number of technical developments, including a common docking system, which had to be specially designed so that the different spacecraft could connect in orbit. The joint mission also gave both "sides" a view of one another's space programs. In preparation for the flight, Soviet cosmonauts and their backups visited and trained at the Johnson Space Center, and the American crew and their backups paid visits to Moscow. Flight controllers from both nations also conducted joint simulations.

Although Apollo-*Soyuz* was a one-time-only event, it created a sense of goodwill that transcended the simple "handshake in space" that was its most visible symbol.

Apollo-Soyuz Statistics

Date: 1975

Vehicles: Saturn IB launcher, Apollo Command Module

Number of People Flown: 3

Total Time in Space: 9 days

Highlights: First international space mission

Bibliography

NASA Sources

Ezell, Edward Clinton, and Linda Neuman Ezell. *The Partnership: A History of the Apollo Soyuz Test Project.* NASA SP-4209, 1978. Available online at *http://history.nasa.gov/SP-4209/cover.htm*.

NASA History Division Apollo-*Soyuz* 30th Anniversary Web site: *http://history.nasa.gov/30thastp/index.html*.

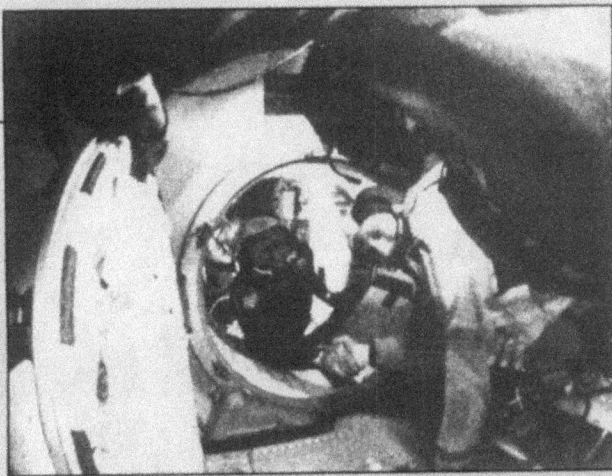

The Apollo commander, astronaut Thomas P. Stafford (in foreground), and the *Soyuz* commander, cosmonaut Alexei A. Leonov, make their historic handshake in space during the joint Russian-American docking mission known as the ASTP, or Apollo-*Soyuz* Test Project. (S75-29432)

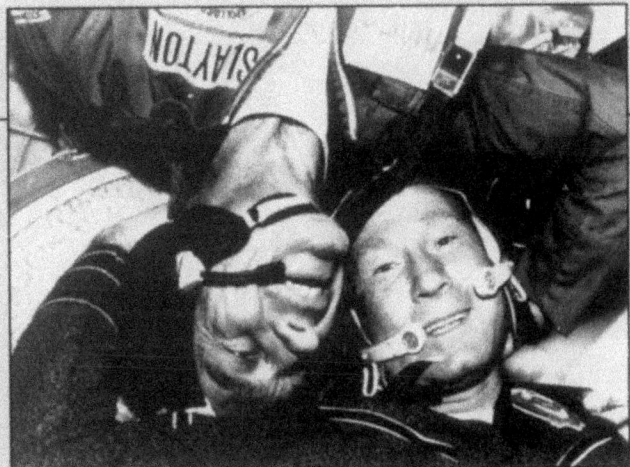

Astronaut Deke Slayton (left) and cosmonaut Aleksei Leonov are photographed together in the *Soyuz* Orbital Module during the joint U.S.-USSR ASTP docking in Earth orbit. (AST-05-298)

Apollo-*Soyuz* Mission

Apollo-*Soyuz* Test Project (ASTP)
15–24 July 1975
Crew: Thomas P. Stafford, Jr., Vance D. Brand,
　　　　Donald K. "Deke" Slayton

The *Soyuz* 19 and Apollo 18 craft launched within 7.5 hours of each other on 15 July and docked on 17 July. Three hours later, Thomas Stafford and Alexei Leonov exchanged the first international handshake in space through the open hatch of the *Soyuz*. The two spacecraft remained linked for 44 hours, long enough for the three Americans and two Soviets to exchange flags and gifts (including tree seeds that were later planted in the two countries), sign certificates, pay visits to each other's ships, eat together, and converse in each other's languages. There were also docking and redocking maneuvers, during which the *Soyuz* reversed roles and became the "active" spacecraft. The Soviets remained in space for five days and the Americans for nine, during which time the Soviets also conducted experiments in Earth observation.

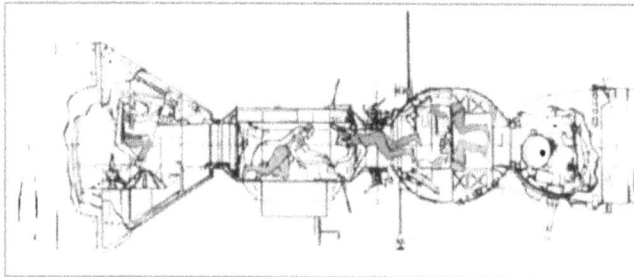

Internal arrangement of docked configuration. (S74-05269)

Artist's concept of Apollo-*Soyuz*. (MSFC-73A-S1905B)

Dawn breaks behind the ASTP Saturn IB launch vehicle during the Countdown Demonstration Test. (75PC-0332)

SPACE SHUTTLE

Overview

Before the Space Shuttle, launching cargo into space was a one-way proposition. Satellites could be sent into orbit, but they could not return. The world's first reusable space vehicle changed that and revolutionized the way people worked in space.

The Space Shuttle was approved as a national program in 1972. Part spacecraft and part aircraft, the Shuttle required several technological advances, including thousands of insulating tiles able to stand the heat of reentry over the course of many missions and sophisticated engines (Space Shuttle Main Engines [SSMEs]) that could be used again and again without being thrown away.

The airplane-like orbiter has three of these SSMEs, which burn liquid hydrogen and oxygen stored in the large External Tank (ET), the single largest structure in the Shuttle "stack." Attached to the tank are two Solid Rocket Boosters (SRBs), which provide most of the vehicle's thrust at liftoff. Two minutes into the flight, the spent SRBs drop into the ocean to be recovered, while the orbiter's own engines continue burning until approximately 8 minutes into the flight.

The Shuttle was developed throughout the 1970s. *Enterprise*, a test vehicle not suited for spaceflight, was used for the approach and landing tests in 1977 that demonstrated the orbiter's aerodynamic qualities and ability to land (after separating from an airplane). The first spaceworthy Shuttle orbiter, *Columbia*, made its orbital debut in April 1981.

The first four missions of the new Space Transportation System (STS) were test flights to evaluate the Shuttle's engineering design, thermal characteristics, and performance in space. Operational flights began with STS-5 in November 1982, with a four-person crew on board. Over time, the crews grew in size: five people flew on STS-7 in 1983 and six on STS-9 later that same year. The first seven-person crew flew on STS-41C in 1984, and in 1985, eight people—a Shuttle record—flew on STS-61A.

The Space Shuttle changed the sociology of spaceflight. With such large crews, Shuttle astronauts were divided into two categories: pilots, responsible for flying and maintaining the orbiter, and mission specialists, responsible for experiments and payloads. A new class of space traveler, payload specialists (who are not even necessarily career astronauts), was also created to tend to specific on-board experiments.

The reusable Shuttles together make up a fleet, with each vehicle continually being processed on the ground in preparation for its next flight. The second orbiter, *Challenger*, debuted in 1983, followed by *Discovery* in 1984 and *Atlantis* in 1985. The *Challenger* orbiter was destroyed and the seven-member crew of STS-51L died when the vehicle exploded 73 seconds after liftoff on 28 January 1986. A fifth orbiter, *Endeavour*, joined the fleet in 1991 to replace *Challenger*.

The Space Transportation System introduced several new tools to the business of spaceflight. The Remote Manipulator System (RMS), a 15.24-meter (50-foot) crane built by the Canadian Space Agency (CSA) and designed to mimic the human arm, is able to move large and heavy payloads in and out of the Shuttle's 18.29-meter-long (60-foot-long) cargo bay.

A cloud of extremely hot steam boils out of the flame deflector at the A-1 test stand during a test firing of a Space Shuttle Main Engine (SSME) at the John C. Stennis Space Center, Hancock County, Mississippi. (88-072-11)

A remote camera captures a close-up view of a Space Shuttle Main Engine during a test firing at Stennis. (GPN-2000-000543)

The Spacelab module, built by the European Space Agency (ESA), provides a pressurized and fully equipped laboratory for scientists to conduct experiments ranging in subject matter from astronomy to materials science to biomedical investigations. The Manned Maneuvering Unit (MMU) backpack allows spacewalking astronauts to "fly" up to several hundred meters from the orbiter with no connecting tether.

The MMU has figured in several of the Shuttle program's most spectacular accomplishments. On STS-41C in April 1984, the ailing Solar Max satellite was retrieved, repaired, and reorbited by the astronaut crew, all on the same flight. Later that same year, on STS-51A, two malfunctioning commercial communications satellites were retrieved in orbit and brought back to Earth in the Shuttle cargo bay. Another malfunctioning satellite was fixed in orbit by the crew of STS-51I in 1985.

Early in the Shuttle program, communications satellites were common payloads, with as many as three delivered into orbit on the same mission. The January 1986 *Challenger* accident, which resulted in the loss of the crew and vehicle due to a failed seal in one of the two Solid Rocket Boosters, led to a change in that policy, however. Since returning to flight in September 1988, the Shuttle has carried only those payloads unique to the Shuttle or those that require a human presence. Most of these payloads have been scientific and defense missions. Among those payloads have been some of the decade's most important space science projects, including the Hubble Space Telescope (HST), the Galileo Jupiter spacecraft, and the Gamma Ray Observatory (GRO).

In 1995, the Shuttle program added a new capability to its repertoire. In preparation for deployment of the International Space Station (ISS), the crew of the Space Shuttle began a series of eight dockings and five crew exchanges with the Russian space station *Mir*. U.S. astronauts spent time aboard *Mir*—sometimes several months at a time—acclimating themselves to living and working in space. They carried out many of the types of activities they would perform on the Space Station and simulated conditions they would possibly encounter.

The Shuttle would be an instrumental participant in another orbital outpost, the International Space Station. The Space Transportation System would be called upon as the major workhorse for the assembly of the ISS, bringing major parts to orbit and carrying the crews that would inhabit the research facility.

Shuttle flights to build the ISS and conduct other tasks continued smoothly until 1 February 2003. As the crew of STS-107 reentered Earth's atmosphere, their *Columbia* orbiter became engulfed in flames and broke apart over the western United States. NASA immediately grounded the Shuttle fleet and commissioned the Columbia Accident Investigation Board to conduct an inquiry into the disaster. Investigators found that upon launch of STS-107, a piece of foam from the External Tank fell onto *Columbia*'s underside and cracked a heatshield tile. This damage later allowed hot gases from reentry to penetrate the structure of the Shuttle.

To resume spaceflights, NASA conducted modifications to the External Tank, including using additional cameras to document liftoff, a new foam application procedure, and other redesigned structures. Additionally, missions were limited to daytime launches, and, once in orbit, an extensive survey of the Shuttle's thermal tiles with a boom attached to the spacecraft's robotic arm was required. Following modi-

Space Shuttle *Enterprise* is lifted into the Dynamic Test Stand. (7992403)

The orbiter *Enterprise* turns and banks during the second approach and landing test. (ECN-8607)

fications to the External Tank, the Space Shuttle returned to flight on 26 July 2005 with STS-114. While regular flights to the Station resumed after another year of modifications in summer 2006, the Space Transportation System is slated for retirement by 2010.

As of STS-116, the Space Shuttle has flown 305 men and women into orbit during 117 missions into space. The Shuttle had also logged approximately 1,082 days, 7 hours, and 49 minutes in space and performed 17,331 Earth orbits.

Space Shuttle Statistics

Dates: 1981–present

Vehicles: Space Shuttle orbiter, External Tank, Solid Rocket Boosters

Number of People Flown (not counting astronauts who have flown several times): 305 (through December 2006)

Orbiter Fleet (OV = Orbiter Vehicle):
Enterprise (OV-101, test vehicle, no spaceflight; status: property of National Air and Space Museum)
Columbia (OV-102; status: vehicle lost during reentry on mission STS-107, 1 February 2003)
Challenger (OV-099; status: vehicle lost during STS-51L launch on 28 January 1986)
Discovery (OV-103; status: active)
Atlantis (OV-104; status: active)
Endeavour (OV-105; status: active)

Highlights: First reusable spacecraft, first in-space satellite repairs and retrievals

Bibliography

NASA Sources

Allaway, Howard. *The Space Shuttle at Work*. NASA SP-432/EP-156, 1979. Available online at *http://history.nasa.gov/SP-432/sp432.htm*.

Froelich, Walter. *Spacelab: An International Short-Stay Orbiting Laboratory*. NASA EP-165. Available online at *http://history.nasa.gov/EP-165/ep165.htm*.

Guilmartin, John F., and John Maurer. *A Space Shuttle Chronology*. NASA Johnson Space Center, 1988.

Heppenheimer, T. A. *The Space Shuttle Decision: NASA's Search for a Reusable Space Vehicle*. NASA SP-4221, 1999. Available online at *http://history.nasa.gov/SP-4221/sp4221.htm*.

Launius, Roger D., and Aaron K. Gillette, comps. *Toward a History of the Space Shuttle: An Annotated Bibliography*. Monographs in Aerospace History, No. 1, 1992. Available online at *http://history.nasa.gov/Shuttlebib/cover.html*.

NASA Space Shuttle Reference Web site, *http://spaceflight.nasa.gov/shuttle/reference/*.

Science in Orbit: The Shuttle & Spacelab Experience: 1981–1986. NASA NP-119, Marshall Space Flight Center, 1988. Available online at *http://history.nasa.gov/NP-119/NP-119.htm*.

The Space Shuttle. NASA SP-407, 1976. Available online at *http://history.nasa.gov/SP-407/sp407.htm*.

STS-1 crew members: John Young, commander, and Robert Crippen, pilot. (S79-31775)

Launch view of *Columbia* for the STS-1 mission on 12 April 1981. (81PC-0373)

Non-NASA Sources

Allen, Joseph. *Entering Space.* Stewart, Tabori & Chang, 1984.

Cooper, Henry S. F., Jr. *Before Liftoff: The Making of a Space Shuttle Crew.* Johns Hopkins University Press, 1987.

Evans, Ben. *Space Shuttle Challenger: Ten Journeys into the Unknown.* Springer/Praxis, 2007.

———. *Space Shuttle Columbia: Her Missions and Crews.* Springer/Praxis, 2005.

Forres, George. *Space Shuttle: The Quest Continues.* Ian Allen, 1989.

Furniss, Tim. *Space Shuttle Log.* Jane's, 1986.

Gurney, Gene, and Jeff Forte. *The Space Shuttle Log: The First 25 Flights.* Aero Books, 1988.

Harland, David M. *The Space Shuttle: Roles, Missions, Accomplishments.* John Wiley & Sons/Praxis, 1998.

———. *The Story of the Space Shuttle.* Springer-Verlag/Praxis, 2004.

Jenkins, Dennis. *Space Shuttle: The History of the National Space Transportation System: The First 100 Missions.* 3rd edition. Dennis Jenkins, 2001.

Joels, Kerry Mark, and Greg Kennedy. *Space Shuttle Operator's Manual.* Ballantine Books, 1982.

Lewis, Richard S. *The Last Voyage of Challenger.* Columbia University Press, 1988.

———. *The Voyages of Columbia: The First True Spaceship.* Columbia University Press, 1984.

Nelson, Bill, with Jamie Buckingham. *Mission: An American Congressman's Voyage to Space.* Harcourt, Brace, Jovanovich, 1988.

Stockton, William, and John Noble Wilford. *Spaceliner: Report on Columbia's Voyage into Tomorrow.* Times Books, 1981.

Useful Shuttle Web Sites

Shuttle History: *http://history.nasa.gov/shuttlehistory.html*

Pre-Mission Information (Shuttle press kits):

> Recent Missions: *http://www.shuttlepresskit.com/index.html*

> Older Missions: *http://www.jsc.nasa.gov/history/shuttle_pk/shuttle_press.htm*

Shuttle Mission Summaries (postflight): *http://www.nasa.gov/mission_pages/shuttle/shuttlemissions/list_main.html*

Shuttle-*Mir*: *http://spaceflight1.nasa.gov/history/shuttle-mir/*

Shuttle Images/Audio/Video: *http://spaceflight.nasa.gov/gallery/images/shuttle/index.html*

Shuttle Images (early flights): *http://images.jsc.nasa.gov/*

NASA Shuttle Home Page: *http://www.nasa.gov/mission_pages/shuttle/main/index.html*

STS-1 25th Anniversary Web Site: *http://history.nasa.gov/sts25th/index.htm*

Challenger STS-51L Accident Web Site: *http://history.nasa.gov/sts51l.html*

Columbia STS-107 Accident Web Site: *http://history.nasa.gov/columbia/index.html*

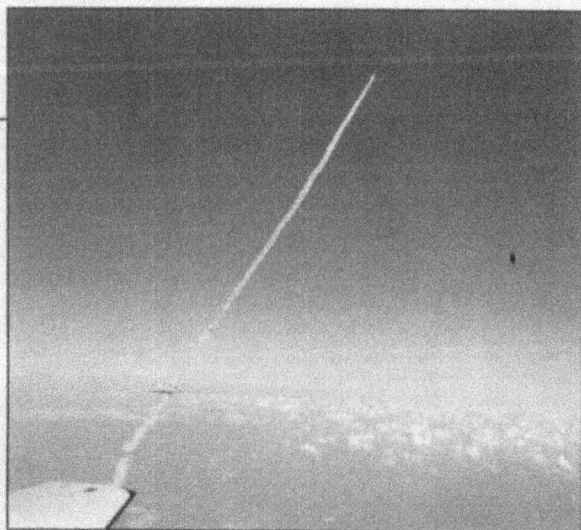

This photograph of *Columbia* soaring toward Earth orbit at the beginning of STS-2 was captured by astronaut and mission specialist Kathryn Sullivan from the rear station of a T-38 jet aircraft. (S81-39527)

Huge crowds flocked to a public viewing site on the east shore of Rogers Dry Lake to watch the first Space Shuttle landing. (http://www.nasa.gov/images/content/145977main1_sts1_camping.jpg)

Shuttle Missions

Note: Cdr = Commander; MS = Mission Specialist; PS = Payload Specialist; PC= Payload Commander

Foreign (Non-NASA) Space Agencies: AEB = Agência Espacial Brasileira (Brazilian Space Agency); ASI = Agenzia Spaziale Italiana (Italian Space Agency); CNES = Centre National d'Études Spatiales (French Space Agency); CSA = Canadian Space Agency; ESA = European Space Agency; NASDA = National Space and Development Agency (Japanese Space Agency), now called JAXA = Japan Aerospace Exploration Agency; NSAU = National Space Agency of Ukraine; RSA = Russian Space Agency; RSC Energia = Rocket & Space Corporation Energia (Russia)

STS-1 (First Shuttle flight)
12–14 April 1981
Columbia (First flight)
Crew: John W. Young (Cdr) and Robert L.
   Crippen (Pilot)

On its debut flight, the Space Shuttle proved that it could safely reach Earth orbit and return through the atmosphere to land like an airplane. In space, John Young and Robert Crippen tested *Columbia*'s on-board systems; fired the Orbital Maneuvering System (OMS) used for changing orbits and the Reaction Control System (RCS) engines used for attitude control; opened and closed the payload bay doors (the bay was empty for this first flight); and, after 36 orbits, made a smooth touchdown at Edwards Air Force Base in California, the landing site for most of the early Shuttle missions. STS-1 was the first time a crewed space vehicle was tested with people on board and the first time that a human-rated spacecraft used solid propellant as fuel. Shock waves from the ignition of the Space Shuttle Main Engines caused damage to the orbiter's thermal tiles.

STS-2 (Second Shuttle flight)
12–14 November 1981
Columbia (Second flight)
Crew: Joe H. Engle (Cdr) and Richard H.
   Truly (Pilot)

Originally intended to last five days, the Shuttle's second test flight was cut short when problems developed with one of three on-board fuel cells that produce electricity. Joe Engle and Richard Truly conducted the first tests of the 15.24-meter (50-foot) Remote Manipulator System arm and operated the Shuttle's first payload: a package of Earth-viewing instruments stored in the cargo bay. A sound-suppressing system was installed to eliminate the problem created by the Shuttle's main engine's shock wave at ignition.

STS-3 (Third Shuttle flight)
22–30 March 1982
Columbia (Third flight)
Crew: Jack R. Lousma (Cdr) and Charles G. "Gordo"
   Fullerton (Pilot)

The longest of the Shuttle test flights, STS-3 carried space-viewing instruments for the first time. The crew also continued engineering evaluations of *Columbia*. After rains flooded the dry lakebed at the primary landing site in California, *Columbia* made the Shuttle program's first landing at White Sands, New Mexico.

Space Shuttle *Columbia*'s first landing was at NASA's Dryden Flight Research Center, Edwards Air Force Base, California. (http://www.nasa.gov/images/content/145978main2_sts1_landing.jpg)

Space Shuttle *Columbia* on Rogers Dry Lake at Edwards AFB after completing its first orbital mission on 14 April 1981. (S81-31163)

STS-4 (Fourth Shuttle flight)
27 June–4 July 1982
Columbia (Fourth flight)
Crew: Thomas K. Mattingly II (Cdr) and Henry W.
  "Hank" Hartsfield (Pilot)

The last Shuttle test flight was the first mission to carry pay-loads for the Department of Defense. It also included the first small "Get-Away Special" experiments mounted in the cargo bay and further tested the mechanical and thermal performance of *Columbia* as well as the environment surrounding the spacecraft. Thomas Mattingly made the first Shuttle landing on a concrete runway instead of the dry lakebed at Edwards Air Force Base.

STS-5 (Fifth Shuttle flight)
11–16 November 1982
Columbia (Fifth flight)
Crew: Vance D. Brand (Cdr), Robert F. Overmyer
  (Pilot), Joseph P. Allen (MS1), William B.
  Lenoir (MS2)

The Shuttle's first operational mission also was the first spaceflight with four people on board. Two commercial communications satellites, SBS-3 and Anik C-3, were launched into orbit from the cargo bay (another first) using the Payload Assist Module (PAM) upper stage designed for the Shuttle. A planned spacewalk was canceled when problems developed with the two on-board spacesuits.

STS-6 (Sixth Shuttle flight)
4–9 April 1983
Challenger (First flight)

Crew: Paul J. Weitz (Cdr), Karol J. Bobko (Pilot),
  F. Story Musgrave (MS1), Donald H.
  Peterson (MS2)

Challenger's debut flight included the Shuttle program's first spacewalks. Story Musgrave and Donald Peterson spent more than 4 hours testing new Shuttle spacesuits and mobility aids and evaluated their own ability to work outside in the Shuttle's cargo bay. The first of NASA's Tracking and Data Relay Satellites (TDRS) was launched. The communications satellite initially failed to reach its proper orbit because of an upper stage guidance error, but it was eventually maneuvered into the correct position.

STS-7 (Seventh Shuttle flight)
18–24 June 1983
Challenger (Second flight)
Crew: Robert L. Crippen (Cdr), Frederick H. "Rick"
  Hauck (Pilot), John M. Fabian (MS1), Sally K.
  Ride (MS2), Norman E. Thagard (MS3)

Except for Robert Crippen, all the members of this crew were from the "class" of 1978, the first astronauts chosen for the Shuttle program. STS-7 had a record five people on board, including Sally Ride, the first American woman in space. The crew deployed, rendezvoused with, and retrieved the German-built Shuttle Pallet Satellite (SPAS) experiment platform, which took the first full pictures of a Shuttle orbiter in space. The crew also released two communications satellites, Anik C-2 and Palapa B-l, into orbit and activated a series of materials processing experiments fixed in *Challenger's* cargo bay.

View of *Columbia's* RMS arm and end effector grasping the Induced Environment Contamination Monitor (IECM) during STS-4. (*http://science.ksc.nasa.gov/mirrors/images/ pao/STS4/10060812.jpg*)

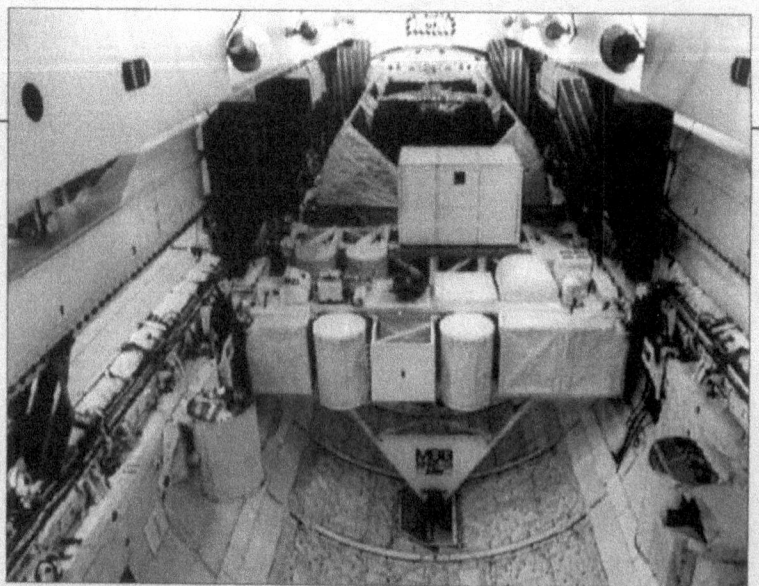

A view of the cargo bay of the orbiter *Challenger* at launch facility 39A, with the STS-7 payload in position. (S83-33870)

STS-8 (Eighth Shuttle flight)
30 August–5 September 1983
Challenger (Third flight)
Crew: Richard H. Truly (Cdr), Daniel C. Brandenstein
(Pilot), Dale A. Gardner (MS1), Guion S.
Bluford (MS2), William E. Thornton (MS3)

STS-8 featured the Shuttle program's first night launch and landing. The crew launched India's Insat 1-B communications satellite, conducted the first tests of Shuttle-to-ground communications with the new Tracking and Data Relay Satellites, and exercised the Remote Manipulator System arm with a test article weighing nearly 3,383.8 kilograms (7,460 pounds). William Thornton, a doctor of medicine (M.D.), conducted biomedical experiments, and Guion Bluford became the first African American in space.

STS-9 (Ninth Shuttle flight)
28 November–8 December 1983
Columbia (Sixth flight)
Crew: John W. Young (Cdr); Brewster H. Shaw, Jr.
(Pilot); Owen K. Garriott (MS1); Robert A. R.
Parker (MS2); Ulf D. Merbold (PS1), ESA
(Germany); Byron K. Lichtenberg (PS2)

The first flight of the European-built Spacelab module was a multidisciplinary science mission, with 73 experiments in a wide range of fields, including space physics, materials processing, life sciences, Earth and atmospheric studies, astronomy, and solar physics. The record six-person crew included the first Shuttle payload specialists: Byron Lichtenberg of Massachusetts Institute of Technology (MIT) and Ulf Merbold, a West German physicist who became the first non-U.S. citizen to fly on an American spacecraft.

STS-41B (10th Shuttle flight)
3–11 February 1984
Challenger (Fourth flight)
Crew: Vance D. Brand (Cdr), Robert L. "Hoot"
Gibson (Pilot), Ronald E. McNair (MS1),
Robert L. Stewart (MS2), Bruce
McCandless II (MS3)

With this flight, the number designations for Shuttle missions changed. The "4" indicates the (originally scheduled) year of the launch, 1984. The second digit represents the launch site ("1" for Florida, "2" for California), and the "B" indicates the second launch of the fiscal year. The first-ever untethered spacewalks were performed by Bruce McCandless and Robert Stewart, who tested new Manned Maneuvering Unit backpacks that allowed them to travel as far as almost 97.54 meters (320 feet) from the orbiter. Two satellites deployed from the Shuttle, Westar V-I and Palapa B-2, failed to reach their proper orbits when their Payload Assist Module upper stages did not ignite. Both were later retrieved and brought back to Earth (see STS-51A). *Challenger* made the Shuttle's first landing at the Kennedy Space Center in Florida.

STS-41C (11th Shuttle flight)
6–13 April 1984
Challenger (Fifth flight)
Crew: Robert L. Crippen (Cdr), Francis R. "Dick"
Scobee (Pilot), Terry J. Hart (MS1), James D.
van Hoften (MS2), George D. Nelson (MS3)

In the space program's first satellite service call, the crew rendezvoused with and retrieved the Solar Maximum Mission (Solar Max) satellite, which had failed after four

Astronaut Bruce McCandless, mission specialist, participates in an extravehicular activity (EVA) during STS-41B. He is using a nitrogen-propelled, hand-controlled manned maneuvering unit (MMU). He is performing this EVA without being tethered to the Shuttle and is approaching his maximum distance from *Challenger*. Below him is a cloudy view of Earth. (S84-27019)

STS-41C mission specialists repair the captured Solar Maximum Mission Satellite. (STS41C-37-1711)

years in orbit. With the satellite anchored in *Challenger*'s cargo bay, George Nelson and James van Hoften replaced a faulty attitude control system and one science instrument, and the repaired satellite was re-released into orbit. The Long Duration Exposure Facility (LDEF), a passive satellite for testing the effects of space exposure on different materials, also was deployed on the flight. Originally, the LDEF was to have remained in orbit for only 10 months, but it was not returned to Earth until STS-32 in January 1990 due to the *Challenger* accident (see STS-51L).

STS-41D (12th Shuttle flight)
30 August–5 September 1984
Discovery (First flight)
Crew: Henry W. "Hank" Hartsfield (Cdr), Michael L.
     Coats (Pilot), Richard M. Mullane (MS1),
     Steven A. Hawley (MS2), Judith A.
     Resnick (MS3), Charles D. Walker (PS1)

The first flight of *Discovery* was the first Shuttle mission to deploy three communications satellites: Syncom IV-2, SBS-4, and TELSTAR 3-C. The crew also experimented with a 31.09-meter-high (102-foot-high) solar cell array, which was unfurled from a stowage container only 177.8 millimeters (7 inches) deep, located in the cargo bay. The experiments included testing the structure's stability when the Shuttle's attitude control engines were fired. Charles Walker, a McDonnell Douglas engineer, was the Shuttle's first commercially sponsored payload specialist, on board to tend to the company's Continuous Flow Electrophoresis System for separating materials in microgravity.

STS-41G (13th Shuttle flight)
5–13 October 1984
Challenger (Sixth flight)

Crew: Robert L. Crippen (Cdr); Jon A. McBride (Pilot);
     Kathryn D. Sullivan (MS1); Sally K. Ride (MS2);
     David C. Leestma (MS3); Paul D. Scully-Power
     (PS1); Marc Garneau (PS2), CSA (Canada)

The Shuttle's first seven-member crew included two payload specialists: Paul Scully-Power, a Navy oceanographer, was on board to observe ocean dynamics from orbit, and Marc Garneau, the first Canadian in space, operated the multidisciplinary CANEX (Canadian Experiment) package. In *Challenger*'s cargo bay was a suite of instruments dedicated to Earth observation, the primary purpose of this mission. During a 3.5-hour spacewalk, Kathryn Sullivan and David Leestma also tested connections for an orbital refueling system in the bay. Sullivan was the first American woman to walk in space.

STS-51A (14th Shuttle flight)
8–16 November 1984
Discovery (Second flight)
Crew: Frederick H. "Rick" Hauck (Cdr), David M.
     Walker (Pilot), Joseph P. Allen (MS1), Dale A.
     Gardner (MS3)

The STS-51A crew delivered two satellites, Anik D-2 and Syncom IV-I, into orbit, then brought two others, Palapa B-2 and Westar V-I, whose on-board boosters had failed after being deployed on STS-41B, back to Earth. In separate spacewalks using Manned Maneuvering Unit backpacks, Dale Gardner and Joseph Allen each docked with an orbiting satellite, stopped its rotation, then assisted as it was stowed in *Discovery*'s cargo bay. Both satellites were then returned for refurbishment on the ground in a dramatic demonstration of the Shuttle's salvage capability.

Astronaut Kathryn Sullivan checks the latch of the SIR-B antenna in *Challenger*'s open cargo bay during STS-41G. The orbital refueling system (ORS) is just beyond the mission specialist's helmet. To the left is the large format camera (LFC). The LFC and ORS are stationed on a device called the mission peculiar experiment support structure (MPESS). (STS41G-13-032)

Astronauts Dale Gardner and Joseph Allen during the loading of Palapa B-2 into the payload bay on mission STS-51A. (STS51A-41-058)

STS-51C (15th Shuttle flight)
24–27 January 1985
Discovery (Third flight)
Crew: Thomas K. Mattingly II (Cdr), Loren J.
       Shriver (Pilot), Ellison S. Onizuka (MS1),
       James F. Buchli (MS2), Gary E. Payton (PS1)

The crew for the Shuttle's first flight dedicated to the Department of Defense included payload specialist Gary Payton of the U.S. Air Force. The cargo and details of the mission are classified.

STS-51D (16th Shuttle flight)
12–19 April 1985
Discovery (Fourth flight)
Crew: Karol J. Bobko (Cdr), Donald E. Williams
       (Pilot), Margaret R. Seddon (MS1), Stanley D.
       Griggs (MS2), Jeffrey A. Hoffman (MS3),
       Charles D. Walker (PS1), E. Jacob Garn (PS2)

When a booster attached to Syncom IV-3, the second of two communications satellites released into orbit (the other was Anik C-l), failed to ignite, the crew, with the help of engineers on the ground, attempted a fix. Jeffrey Hoffman and Stanley Griggs took an unscheduled spacewalk to attach an improvised "flyswatter" device to the Remote Manipulator System arm in the hope that it could trip the satellite booster's sequence start lever. The plan failed, however, and the satellite was eventually "jump-started" by STS-51I astronauts four months later. Utah Senator Jake Garn was the first member of Congress to fly in space.

STS-51B (17th Shuttle flight)
29 April–6 May 1985
Challenger (Seventh flight)
Crew: Robert F. Overmyer (Cdr), Frederick D.
       Gregory (Pilot), Don L. Lind (MS1), Norman
       E. Thagard (MS2), William E. Thornton (MS3),
       Taylor G. Wang (PS1), Lodewijk van den Berg
       (PS2)

The Shuttle's second Spacelab mission included 15 experiments in topics including materials processing, fluid behavior, atmospheric physics, astronomy, and life sciences. The crew worked around the clock in shifts. They also had trouble with a leaky animal-holding facility that was making its first test flight. Taylor Wang, a Jet Propulsion Laboratory (JPL) scientist, concentrated on studies of fluid behavior in microgravity, while Lodewijk van den Berg of EG&G, Inc., focused on crystal growth experiments. Don Lind, an astronaut since 1966, made his first spaceflight.

STS-51G (18th Shuttle flight)
17–24 June 1985
Discovery (Fifth flight)
Crew: Daniel C. Brandenstein (Cdr); John O.
       Creighton (Pilot); John M. Fabian (MS1);
       Steven R. Nagel (MS2); Shannon W. Lucid
       (MS3); Sultan Abdul Aziz Al-Saud (PS1),
       Saudi Arabia; Patrick Baudry (PS2),
       CNES (France)

Patrick Baudry of France and Sultan Abdul Aziz Al-Saud of Saudi Arabia were the international payload specialists for this flight, which successfully launched three commu-

Mission specialist Ellison Onizuka, wearing the Kamakze headband, appears to be keeping a sleeping Loren Shriver, pilot, from floating in his sleep restraints through the middeck of *Discovery* during the STS-51C mission. (STS51C-08-035)

A drop centered in this 35mm frame served as a test subject for the principal investigator of the Drop Dynamics Module Experiment on mission STS-51B. (STS51B-14-037)

nications satellites into orbit: MORELOS 1, ARABSAT 1-B, and TELSTAR 3-D. Shuttle Pointed Autonomous Research Tool for Astronomy (SPARTAN-I), a reusable, free-flying payload carrier with astronomy instruments on board, also was released then retrieved by the Remote Manipulator System arm. The crew conducted materials science and biomedical experiments and participated in a Defense Department tracking experiment in which a laser beam directed from Hawaii was bounced from a reflector on board *Discovery* back to the ground.

STS-51F (19th Shuttle flight)
29 July–6 August 1985
Challenger (Eighth flight)
Crew: Charles G. "Gordo" Fullerton (Cdr), Roy D.
    Bridges (Pilot), Karl G. Henize (MS1),
    F. Story Musgrave (MS2), Anthony W.
    England (MS3), Loren W. Acton (PS1),
    John-David F. Bartoe (PS2)

The Spacelab 2 mission replaced the Spacelab's enclosed "long module" with open pallets containing 13 instruments dedicated to astronomy. Despite problems with an instrument pointing system, the crew was able to collect data on the Sun and other celestial targets. Earlier in the flight, *Challenger* made the Shuttle program's first "abort to orbit" when one of its three main engines shut down during the ascent. Karl Henize and Anthony England had waited a long time for a spaceflight—both were astronauts during the Apollo era. England had resigned from NASA in 1972, only to rejoin the astronaut corps in 1979.

STS-51I (20th Shuttle flight)
27 August–3 September 1985

Discovery (Sixth flight)
Crew: Joe H. Engle (Cdr), Richard O. Covey (Pilot),
    James D. van Hoften (MS1), John M. "Mike"
    Lounge (MS2), William F. Fisher (MS3)

The Syncom IV-3 satellite (also known as "Leasat"), stranded in orbit on STS-51D, was repaired and reboosted as a result of two spacewalks by James van Hoften and William Fisher that were among the most challenging in the history of the space program. After van Hoften, standing on the end of the Remote Manipulator System arm, grabbed the satellite manually, he and Fisher worked on the satellite in *Discovery*'s cargo bay. The astronauts attached hardware that allowed ground crews to activate Syncom's still-live rocket motor after van Hoften re-released it into orbit with a shove from the cargo bay. Earlier in the flight, the crew had launched three new communications satellites into orbit: ASC 1, AUSSAT I, and Syncom IV-4 (which was nearly identical to the one that was rescued).

STS-51J (21st Shuttle flight)
3–7 October 1985
Atlantis (First flight)
Crew: Karol J. Bobko (Cdr), Ronald J. Grabe (Pilot),
    David C. Hilmers (MS1), Robert L. Stewart
    (MS2), William A. Pailes (PS1)

The first flight of *Atlantis* was the second Shuttle mission dedicated to the Department of Defense. The payload and on-board activities are classified.

STS-61A (22nd Shuttle flight)
30 October–6 November 1985
Challenger (Ninth flight)

Astronaut James van Hoften working with the Syncom IV-3 satellite on mission STS-51I. (STS51I-102-029)

Space Shuttle *Atlantis* is readied for launch on STS-51J in this low-angle night scene at complex 39. (108-KSC-85PC-417).

Payload specialist Wubbo Ockels, a Dutch scientist, crawls from a unique sleeping restraint in the D-1 science module during STS-61A. (STS61A-18-008)

Crew: Henry W. "Hank" Hartsfield (Cdr); Steven R. Nagel (Pilot); Bonnie J. Dunbar (MS1); James F. Buchli (MS2); Guion S. Bluford (MS3); Reinhard Furrer (PS1), Germany; Ernst W. Messerschmid (PS2), Germany; Wubbo J. Ockels (PS3), ESA (the Netherlands)

The Spacelab D-1 mission was the first U.S. manned spaceflight with a primary payload sponsored by another country: West Germany. On board were 76 experiments, including investigations in fluid physics, materials science, plant physiology, and human adaptation to weightlessness. Science experiments were directed from a German Space Operations Center in Oberpfaffenhofen, and two of the payload specialists, Reinhard Furrer and Ernst Messerschmid, were German. With eight people working around the clock in shifts, it was the largest Shuttle crew to date.

STS-61B (23rd Shuttle flight)
26 November–3 December 1985
Atlantis (Second flight)
Crew: Brewster H. Shaw, Jr. (Cdr); Bryan D. O'Connor (Pilot); Jerry L. Ross (MS1); Mary L. Cleave (MS2); Sherwood C. "Woody" Spring (MS3); Charles D. Walker (PS1); Rodolfo N. Vela (PS2), Mexico

After the crew deployed three communications satellites (SATCOM Ku-2, MORELOS 2, and AUSSAT-2) Woody Spring and Jerry Ross conducted the first construction experiments in space, assembling and disassembling two Tinkertoy®-like structures called Experimental Assembly of Structures in Extravehicular Activity (EASE) and Assembly Concept for Construction of Erectable Space Structures (ACCESS) in the cargo bay of *Atlantis*. The two spacewalking astronauts attached beams, nodes, and struts to evaluate different methods of assembling large structures in space. Rodolfo Vela was the first Mexican citizen in orbit, while Charles Walker made his third flight with the commercially sponsored electrophoresis experiment.

STS-61C (24th Shuttle flight)
12–18 January 1986
Columbia (Seventh flight)
Crew: Robert L. "Hoot" Gibson (Cdr), Charles F. Bolden, Jr. (Pilot), George D. Nelson (MS1), Steven A. Hawley (MS2), Franklin R. Chang-Diaz (MS3), Robert J. Cenker (PS1), C. William "Bill" Nelson (PS2)

Florida Representative Bill Nelson was the second member of Congress to fly on the Shuttle. The crew deployed a communications satellite for the RCA company and conducted a number of smaller experiments, including several materials science investigations mounted in the cargo bay of *Columbia*. An attempt to photograph Comet Halley through an overhead window was unsuccessful, however, due to problems with the instrument's battery.

STS-51L (25th Shuttle flight)
28 January 1986
Challenger (10th flight)
Crew: Francis R. "Dick" Scobee (Cdr), Michael J. Smith (Pilot), Ellison S. Onizuka (MS1), Judith A. Resnick (MS2), Ronald E. McNair (MS3), Sharon Christa McAuliffe (Space Flight Participant; PS1), Gregory B. Jarvis (PS2)

Jerry Ross stands on the end of the Remote Manipulator System during a spacewalk on STS-61B. (STS61B-41-019)

Ice on the pad on the day of STS-51L's launch. The ice caused the loss of elasticity in the SRB O-ring seals. (GPN-2004-00011)

Challenger and all seven members of the crew—including Gregory Jarvis, a Hughes employee, and Christa McAuliffe, the designated "Teacher in Space"—were lost 73 seconds into the flight when the vehicle exploded as the result of a leak in one of two Solid Rocket Boosters. The Shuttle program was delayed for nearly three years while the boosters were redesigned and other safety measures were added. A change in U.S. space policy also resulted from the accident—no longer would the Shuttle carry commercial satellites into orbit.

STS-26 (26th Shuttle flight)
29 September–3 October 1988
Discovery (Seventh flight)
Crew: Frederick H. "Rick" Hauck (Cdr), Richard O. Covey (Pilot), John M. "Mike" Lounge (MS1), David C. Hilmers (MS2), George D. Nelson (MS3)

The first Shuttle mission after the *Challenger* accident was a conservative, four-day flight that proved the safety of the redesigned Solid Rocket Boosters. Aboard *Discovery* was the first all-veteran astronaut crew since Apollo 11. During launch and reentry, the astronauts wore new partial-pressure flight suits, and in orbit they practiced using a new emergency escape system. The principal payload was a NASA Tracking and Data Relay Satellite (TRDS) similar to the one lost on STS-51L, which was released into orbit on the first day.

STS-27 (27th Shuttle flight)
2–6 December 1988
Atlantis (Third flight)
Crew: Robert L. "Hoot" Gibson (Cdr), Guy S. Gardner (Pilot), Richard M. Mullane (MS1), Jerry L. Ross (MS2), William M. Shepherd (MS3)

This was a dedicated and classified mission for the Department of Defense.

STS-29 (28th Shuttle flight)
13–18 March 1989
Discovery (Eighth flight)
Crew: Michael L. Coats (Cdr), John E. Blaha (Pilot), Robert C. Springer (MS1), James F. Buchli (MS2), James P. Bagian (MS3)

Six hours into this mission, the crew released the fourth NASA Tracking and Data Relay Satellite into orbit. The astronauts conducted experiments in plant growth, crystal growth, and the human body's adaptation to weightlessness, and tested a new Shuttle "fax" machine. They also took large-format IMAX movie pictures of Earth and returned clear photographs of the jettisoned External Tank in space.

STS-30 (29th Shuttle flight)
4–8 May 1989
Atlantis (Fourth flight)
Crew: David M. Walker (Cdr), Ronald J. Grabe (Pilot), Mark C. Lee (MS1), Norman E. Thagard (MS2), Mary L. Cleave (MS3)

The Space Shuttle program's first launch of a planetary spacecraft came on the first day of the mission, when the Magellan Venus Radar Mapper was released from *Atlantis*'s cargo bay with an Inertial Upper Stage (IUS) booster attached. The booster fired shortly thereafter to send Magellan to Venus, where it arrived in August 1990 to begin an eight-month mapping mission. Secondary experiments after the deployment included crystal growth studies and a search for thunderstorms in the atmosphere below, called the Mesoscale Lightning Experiment.

Space Shuttle *Atlantis* takes flight on its STS-27 mission on 2 December 1988. (8898508)

The Magellan Venus Radar Mapper is released from *Atlantis* during STS-30. (P-34252BC)

STS-28 (30th Shuttle flight)
8–13 August 1989
Columbia (Eighth flight)
Crew: Brewster H. Shaw, Jr. (Cdr), Richard N. Richards
(Pilot), James C. Adamson (MS1), David C.
Leestma (MS2), Mark N. Brown (MS3)

This was a dedicated and classified mission for the Department of Defense.

STS-34 (31st Shuttle flight)
18–23 October 1989
Atlantis (Fifth flight)
Crew: Donald E. Williams (Cdr), Michael J. McCulley
(Pilot), Shannon W. Lucid (MS1), Franklin R.
Chang-Diaz (MS2), Ellen Baker (-Shulman) (MS3)

The Jupiter-bound Galileo spacecraft was the Shuttle's second interplanetary cargo. Galileo's mission got under way during *Atlantis*'s fifth orbit around Earth, when the spacecraft was released from the cargo bay to head toward Venus, where its intrumentation was checked and Venus's clouds were studied. It then continued its voyage to Jupiter. After releasing Galileo, the crew worked on experiments that included materials science, plant growth, and measurements of ozone in the atmosphere.

STS-33 (32nd Shuttle flight)
22–27 November 1989
Discovery (Ninth flight)
Crew: Frederick D. Gregory (Cdr), John E. Blaha
(Pilot), Manley L. "Sonny" Carter (MS1),
F. Story Musgrave (MS2), Kathryn C.
Thornton (MS3)

This was a dedicated and classified mission for the Department of Defense.

STS-32 (33rd Shuttle flight)
9–20 January 1990
Columbia (Ninth flight)
Crew: Daniel C. Brandenstein (Cdr), James D.
Wetherbee (Pilot), Bonnie J. Dunbar (MS1),
Marsha S. Ivins (MS2), G. David Low (MS3)

The Long Duration Exposure Facility (LDEF), released into orbit on STS-41C in 1984, was finally retrieved after nearly six years in space. After rendezvousing with the large, cylindrical satellite—one of the most complicated space rendezvous operations ever—the crew photographed the LDEF in orbit, grappled it with the Remote Manipulator System arm, and then stowed it in the cargo bay of *Columbia*. Scientists who examined the LDEF after landing found evidence of erosion and micrometeorite impacts, as expected. The Syncom IV-5 satellite also was deployed on the mission. Lasting almost 11 days, STS-32 was the longest Shuttle flight to date.

STS-36 (34th Shuttle flight)
28 February–4 March 1990
Atlantis (Sixth flight)
Crew: John O. Creighton (Cdr), John H. Casper
(Pilot), Richard M. Mullane (MS1), David C.
Hilmers (MS2), Pierre J. Thuot (MS3)

This was a dedicated and classified mission for the Department of Defense.

Mission specialist Mark Brown juggles food containers on *Columbia* during STS-28. (10063140)

LDEF retrieval over South America during STS-32. (STS032-85-051)

STS-31 (35th Shuttle flight)
24–29 April 1990
Discovery (10th flight)
Crew: Loren J. Shriver (Cdr), Charles F. Bolden, Jr. (Pilot), Bruce McCandless II (MS1), Steven A. Hawley (MS2), Kathryn D. Sullivan (MS3)

The Hubble Space Telescope, the first large optical telescope ever to be placed above Earth's atmosphere and the first of NASA's Great Observatories, was released into orbit by the Remote Manipulator System arm on the second day of the flight to begin at least a decade of astronomical observations in space. After the telescope was deployed, the astronauts conducted experiments in crystal growth and monitored the radiation environment on board the orbiter. Because of the need to place the telescope above most of the atmosphere, *Discovery* flew the highest Shuttle orbit to date, reaching an altitude of more than 531 kilometers (329.22 statute miles).

STS-41 (36th Shuttle flight)
6–10 October 1990
Discovery (11th flight)
Crew: Richard N. Richards (Cdr), Robert D. Cabana (Pilot), Bruce E. Melnick (MS1), William M. Shepherd (MS2), Thomas D. Akers (MS3)

Deployment of the European Space Agency's Ulysses spacecraft to explore the polar regions of the Sun was the highlight of this four-day mission. On the first day of the flight, the crew sprung Ulysses from *Discovery*'s cargo bay and fired Ulysses's on-board rockets to send the spacecraft toward a gravity assist at Jupiter. After the deployment, the astronauts conducted a number of secondary experiments, including taking measurements of atmospheric ozone, studying the effects of atomic oxygen on spacecraft materials, and evaluating a new "hands-off" voice command system in the Shuttle crew cabin.

STS-38 (37th Shuttle flight)
15–20 November 1990
Atlantis (Seventh flight)
Crew: Richard O. Covey (Cdr), Frank L. Culbertson, Jr. (Pilot), Robert C. Springer (MS1), Carl J. Meade (MS2), Charles D. "Sam" Gemar (MS3)

This was a dedicated and classified mission for the Department of Defense.

STS-35 (38th Shuttle flight)
2–10 December 1990
Columbia (10th flight)
Crew: Vance D. Brand (Cdr), Guy S. Gardner (Pilot), Jeffrey A. Hoffman (MS1), John M. "Mike" Lounge (MS2), Robert A. R. Parker (MS3), Samuel T. Durrance (PS1), Ronald A. Parise (PS2)

STS-35 was the first Spacelab mission since the *Challenger* accident and the first Shuttle flight dedicated to a single discipline: astrophysics. *Discovery* carried a group of astronomical telescopes called ASTRO-1, as well as four mission specialists with Ph.D.'s in astronomy: Jeffrey Hoffman, Robert Parker, Samuel Durrance, and Ronald Parise. Despite several hardware malfunctions, the crew was able to make observations of a wide variety of astronomical targets, from comets to quasars, with particular attention to x-ray and ultraviolet wavelengths.

Kathryn Sullivan on *Discovery*'s flight deck during STS-31. (STS031-101-053)

STS-38 pilot Frank Culbertson (top) and mission specialist Charles Gemar enjoy a meal on *Atlantis*. (STS038-25-023)

STS-37 (39th Shuttle flight)
5–11 April 1991
Atlantis (Eighth flight)
Crew: Steven R. Nagel (Cdr), Kenneth D. Cameron
    (Pilot), Linda M. Godwin (MS1), Jerry L.
    Ross (MS2), Jerome "Jay" Apt (MS3)

The Gamma Ray Observatory (GRO) was released by *Atlantis*'s Remote Manipulator System arm on the third day of the flight, after Jerry Ross and Jay Apt made an unscheduled spacewalk to repair an antenna on the spacecraft. GRO is the second of NASA's four Great Observatories satellites. It was designed for a long-term program of astronomical observations from Earth orbit and was the heaviest science satellite ever launched from the Shuttle. Later in the mission, Ross and Apt returned to the cargo bay to test rail-mounted mechanical push-carts planned for use on Space Station Freedom. These two spacewalks were the first in more than five years.

STS-39 (40th Shuttle flight)
28 April–6 May 1991
Discovery (12th flight)
Crew: Michael L. Coats (Cdr), L. Blaine Hammond
    (Pilot), Gregory J. Harbaugh (MS1), Donald
    R. McMonagle (MS2), Guion S. Bluford (MS3),
    Charles Lacy Veach (MS4), Richard J. Hieb (MS5)

The first unclassified defense-related mission of the Shuttle program included experiments sponsored by the Air Force and the Strategic Defense Initiative (SDI) organization. The studies included extensive infrared, ultraviolet, visible, and x-ray observations of the space environment and the Shuttle itself. On-board instruments also returned high-quality images of Earth's aurora. In an experiment related to ballistic missile defense, *Discovery* released a Shuttle Pallet Satellite instrument platform equipped with infrared sensors to fly in formation and observe rocket thruster plumes as the Shuttle performed a complicated series of maneuvers.

STS-40 (41st Shuttle flight)
5–14 June 1991
Columbia (11th flight)
Crew: Bryan D. O'Connor (Cdr), Sidney M. Gutierrez
    (Pilot), James P. Bagian (MS1), Tamara E.
    Jernigan (MS2), M. Rhea Seddon (MS3),
    F. Andrew "Drew" Gaffney (PS1), Millie E.
    Hughes-Fulford (PS2)

The Spacelab Life Sciences (SLS-1) mission was the first dedicated entirely to understanding the physiological effects of spaceflight. An extensive series of biomedical experiments was conducted on crew members during the nine-day mission, and the results were compared with baseline data collected on the ground before and after the flight. Along with the human subjects, rodents and jellyfish also were on board to be tested for their ability to adapt to microgravity.

STS-43 (42nd Shuttle flight)
2–11 August 1991
Atlantis (Ninth flight)
Crew: John E. Blaha (Cdr), Michael A. Baker (Pilot),
    Shannon W. Lucid (MS1), G. David Low
    (MS2), James C. Adamson (MS3)

This mission marked the first scheduled landing at Kennedy Space Center's Shuttle Landing Facility since January 1986.

STS-35 ASTRO-1 telescopes documented in *Columbia*'s payload bay. (STS035-604-058)

Discovery's reaction control system jets fire during an on-orbit maneuver on STS-39. (STS039-27-016)

The Tracking and Data Relay Satellite-5 (TDRS-5) was the mission's primary payload. The satellite became the fourth member of the orbiting TDRS cluster, which now consisted of two operating satellites plus two spares in the space network.

STS-48 (43rd Shuttle flight)
12–18 September 1991
Discovery (13th flight)
Crew: John O. Creighton (Cdr), Kenneth S. Reightler, Jr., (Pilot), Charles D. "Sam" Gemar (MS1), James F. Buchli (MS2), Mark N. Brown (MS3)

The Upper Atmosphere Research Satellite (UARS) was deployed on this mission. The 6,577.2-kilogram (14,469.8-pound) observatory would investigate the stratosphere, mesosphere, and lower thermosphere. The satellite had 10 sensing and measuring devices for collecting data on particular aspects of the upper atmosphere that could affect the global environment.

STS-44 (44th Shuttle flight)
24 November–1 December 1991
Atlantis (10th flight)
Crew: Frederick D. Gregory (Cdr), Terence T. "Tom" Henricks (Pilot), James S. Voss (MS1), F. Story Musgrave (MS2), Mario Runco, Jr. (MS3), Thomas J. Hennen (PS1)

This unclassified Department of Defense mission deployed the Defense Support Program satellite on the first day of the flight. On-board payloads focused on contamination experiments and medical research.

STS-42 (45th Shuttle flight)
22–30 January 1992
Discovery (14th flight)
Crew: Ronald J. Grabe (Cdr); Stephen S. Oswald (Pilot); Norman E. Thagard (PC-MS1); William F. Readdy (MS2); David C. Hilmers (MS3); Roberta L. Bondar (PS1), CSA (Canada); Ulf D. Merbold (PS2), ESA (Germany)

This mission's primary payload was the International Microgravity Laboratory (IML-1), which made its first flight. Working in the pressurized Spacelab module, the international crew split into two teams for 24-hour research on the human nervous system's adaptation to low gravity and the effects of microgravity on other life forms. The crew also conducted materials processing experiments.

STS-45 (46th Shuttle flight)
24 March–2 April 1992
Atlantis (11th flight)
Crew: Charles F. Bolden, Jr. (Cdr); Brian K. Duffy (Pilot); Kathryn D. Sullivan (PC-MS1); David C. Leestma (MS2); C. Michael Foale (MS3); Dirk D. "Dick" Frimout (PS1), ESA (Belgium); Byron K. Lichtenberg (PS2)

This mission marked the first flight of the Atmospheric Laboratory for Applications and Science-1 (ATLAS-1), which was mounted on non-deployable Spacelab pallets in the orbiter's cargo bay. An international team made up of the United States, France, Germany, Belgium, the United Kingdom, Switzerland, the Netherlands, and Japan provided 12 instruments that performed investigations in the atmospheric sciences.

STS-42 crew members take a look at Earth from *Discovery*'s aft flight deck. (STS042-22-006)

Defense Support Program (DSP)/Inertial Upper Stage spacecraft tilted to predeployment position in *Atlantis*'s payload bay on STS-44. (STS044-71-011)

STS-49 (47th Shuttle flight)
7–16 May 1992
Endeavour (First flight)
Crew: Daniel C. Brandenstein (Cdr), Kevin P. Chilton
(Pilot), Richard J. Hieb (MS1), Bruce E. Melnick
(MS2), Pierre J. Thuot (MS3), Kathryn C.
Thornton (MS4), Thomas D. Akers (MS5)

STS-49 was marked by a number of "firsts." Four space-walks, the most ever on a single mission, highlighted the first voyage of the orbiter *Endeavour*. Two of these were the longest in U.S. spaceflight history to date, with one lasting 8 hours and 29 minutes and the other lasting 7 hours and 45 minutes. The flight also featured the longest spacewalk to date by a female astronaut and was the first spaceflight where three crew members worked outside the spacecraft at the same time. It also was the first time that astronauts attached a live rocket motor to an orbiting satellite. The crew also successfully captured and rede-ployed the Intelsat-VI satellite, which had been stranded in an unusable orbit since its launch in March 1990.

STS-50 (48th Shuttle flight)
25 June–9 July 1992
Columbia (12th flight)
Crew: Richard N. Richards (Cdr), Kenneth D.
Bowersox (Pilot), Bonnie J. Dunbar (MS1),
Ellen Baker (-Shulman) (MS2), Carl J. Meade
(MS3), Lawrence J. DeLucas (PS1), Eugene H.
Trinh (PS2)

The U.S. Microgravity Laboratory-1 (USML-1) made its first flight on this mission. It was the first in a planned series of flights to advance microgravity research efforts in several disciplines. Mission duration surpassed all pre-vious U.S. crewed spaceflights to date with the excep-tion of the three *Skylab* missions in 1973–74. It was the first Shuttle mission equipped with Extended Duration Orbiter (EDO) hardware, which provides additional fuel and allows the Shuttle to remain in orbit for longer peri-ods of time.

STS-46 (49th Shuttle flight)
31 July–8 August 1992
Atlantis (12th flight)
Crew: Loren J. Shriver (Cdr); Andrew M. Allen (Pilot);
Claude Nicollier (MS1), ESA (Switzerland);
Marsha S. Ivins (MS2); Jeffrey A. Hoffman
(PC-MS3); Franklin R. Chang-Diaz (MS4);
Franco A. Malerba (PS1), ASI (Italy)

The primary mission objective was deployment of the European Space Agency's European Retrievable Carrier (EURECA) and operation of the NASA/Italian Space Agency Tethered Satellite System (TSS). After a delay and a shorter-than-planned thruster firing, the satellite was successfully boosted to operational orbit. During TSS deployment, the satellite at the end of the tether reached a distance of only 256 meters (839.68 feet) rather than its planned 20 kilometers (12.4 statute miles) because of a jammed tether line. The satellite it carried was restowed for return to Earth.

The STS-49 crew captures Intelsat VI above *Endeavour*'s payload bay during EVA. (STS049-91-029)

Crew members working on the Spacelab Drop Physics Module, Rack 9, on STS-50. (STS050-02-020)

STS-47 (50th Shuttle flight)
12–20 September 1992
Endeavour (Second flight)
Crew: Robert L. "Hoot" Gibson (Cdr); Curtis L.
        Brown, Jr. (Pilot); Mark C. Lee (MS1); Jerome
        "Jay" Apt (MS2); N. Jan Davis (MS3); Mae C.
        Jemison (MS4); Mamoru M. Mohri (PS1),
        NASDA (Japan)

Spacelab-J, the first Japanese space laboratory, debuted on this flight. Jointly sponsored by NASA and the National Space Development Agency of Japan, the mission included 24 materials science and 20 life sciences experiments. Test subjects included members of the crew, Japanese koi fish, cultured animal and plant cells, chicken embryos, fruit flies, fungi and plant seeds, and frogs and frog eggs. The crew also included the first African American woman to fly in space, Mae Jemison; the first married couple, Mark Lee and Jan Davis; and the first Japanese person to fly on the Shuttle, Mamoru Mohri.

STS-52 (51st Shuttle flight)
22 October–1 November 1992
Columbia (13th flight)
Crew: James D. Wetherbee (Cdr); Michael A. Baker
        (Pilot); Charles Lacy Veach (MS1); William M.
        Shepherd (MS2); Tamara E. Jernigan (MS3);
        Steven G. MacLean (PS1), CSA (Canada)

This mission deployed the Laser Geodynamic Satellite II (LAGEOS), a joint effort of NASA and the Italian Space Agency (ASI), and operated the U.S. Microgravity Payload-1 (USMP-1). The Italian Research Interim Stage (IRIS) was used for the first time to boost LAGEOS into orbit. Studies focused on the influence of gravity on basic fluid and solidification processes.

STS-53 (52nd Shuttle flight)
2–9 December 1992
Discovery (15th flight)
Crew: David M. Walker (Cdr), Robert D. Cabana (Pilot), Guion S. Bluford (MS1), James S. Voss (MS2), Michael R. Clifford (MS3)

This was the last Shuttle flight for the Department of Defense. *Discovery* deployed a classified payload, after which flight activities became unclassified. Ten secondary payloads were contained in or attached to Get-Away Special (GAS) hardware in the cargo bay or located on the middeck.

STS-54 (53rd Shuttle flight)
13–19 January 1993
Endeavour (Third flight)
Crew: John H. Casper (Cdr), Donald R. McMonagle (Pilot), Mario Runco, Jr. (MS1), Gregory J. Harbaugh (MS2), Susan J. Helms (MS3)

The fifth Tracking and Data Relay Satellite (TDRS-F), part of NASA's orbiting communications system, was deployed on this mission. On the fifth day of the flight, mission specialists Mario Runco and Gregory Harbaugh spent almost 5 hours walking in the open payload bay performing a series of extravehicular activity tasks designed to increase NASA's knowledge of working in space. The astronauts tested their abilities to move freely in the cargo bay and climb into foot restraints without using their hands; they also simulated carrying large objects in a

Hurricane Bonnie, seen here northeast of Bermuda in the Atlantic Ocean during STS-47. (STS047-151-618)

During STS-54, Gregory Harbaugh carries Mario Runco during Detailed Test Objective 1210, extravehicular activity operations procedure/training. (STS054-80-000U)

microgravity environment. A Hitchhiker experiment collected data on stars and galactic gases. Hitchhiker experiments are housed in canisters or attached to mounting plates inside the Shuttle's cargo bay and were created to provide a quick reaction and low-cost capability for flying small payloads.

STS-56 (54th Shuttle flight)
8–17 April 1993
Discovery (16th flight)
Crew: Kenneth D. Cameron (Cdr). Stephen S. Oswald (Pilot), C. Michael Foale (MS1), Kenneth D. Cockrell (PC-MS2), Ellen Ochoa (MS3)

The primary payload was the Atmospheric Laboratory for Applications and Science-2 (ATLAS-2), which collected data on the relationship between the Sun's energy output and Earth's middle atmosphere and their effect on the ozone layer. ATLAS-2 was one element of NASA's Mission to Planet Earth program. The crew also used the Remote Manipulator System to deploy the SPARTAN-201, a free-flying science instrument platform that studied velocity and acceleration of solar wind and observed the Sun's corona. Using the Shuttle Amateur Radio Experiment II (SAREX II), the crew also contacted schools around the world and briefly contacted the Russian *Mir* space station, the first contact between the Shuttle and *Mir* using amateur radio equipment.

STS-55 (55th Shuttle flight)
26 April–6 May 1993
Columbia (14th flight)

Crew: Steven R. Nagel (Cdr); Terence T. "Tom" Henricks (Pilot); Jerry L. Ross (MS1); Charles J. Precourt (MS2); Bernard A. Harris, Jr. (MS3); Ulrich Walter (PS1), DARA (Germany); Hans W. Schlegel (PS2), ESA (Germany)

This mission marked the second German Spacelab mission, designated D2. Around-the-clock crews conducted some 88 experiments, covering materials and life sciences, technology applications, Earth observations, astronomy, and atmospheric physics.

STS-57 (56th Shuttle flight)
21 June–1 July 1993
Endeavour (Fourth flight)
Crew: Ronald J. Grabe (Cdr), Brian K. Duffy (Pilot), G. David Low (MS1), Nancy J. Sherlock (MS2), Peter J. K. "Jeff" Wisoff (MS3), Janice E. Voss (MS4)

STS-57 marked the first flight of the commercially developed SPACEHAB, a laboratory designed to more than double pressurized workspace for crew-tended experiments. Altogether, 22 experiments were flown, covering materials and life sciences and a wastewater recycling experiment for the future International Space Station. A 5-hour-and-50-minute spacewalk succeeded in retrieving and stowing the 4,275-kilogram (9,405-pound) EURECA science satellite inside *Endeavour*'s payload bay. The satellite had been deployed on the STS-46 mission in 1992. Two crew members also carried out maneuvers using the robot arm. During the mission, the crew also spoke with President Bill Clinton.

STS-56 view of the free-flying SPARTAN-201 backdropped against heavy cloud cover. (STS056-90-034)

Kenneth Cameron (left) and Stephen Oswald (right) in *Discovery*'s forward flight deck during STS-56. (STS056-39-010)

STS-51 (57th Shuttle flight)
12–22 September 1993
Discovery (17th flight)
Crew: Frank L. Culbertson, Jr. (Cdr), William F.
Readdy (Pilot), James H. Newman (MS1),
Daniel W. Bursch (MS2), Carl E. Walz (MS3)

The Advanced Communications Technology Satellite (ACTS) was deployed on this mission. The attached Transfer Orbit Stage (TOS) booster was used for the first time to propel the communications technology spacecraft to geosynchronous transfer orbit. The second primary payload, the Orbiting and Retrievable Far and Extreme Ultraviolet Spectrograph-Shuttle Pallet Satellite (ORFEUS-SPAS), first in a series of Astronomical-SPAS (ASTRO-SPAS) astronomical missions, was also deployed. The joint German-U.S. astrophysics payload was controlled from the SPAS Payload Operations Control Center at Kennedy Space Center, the first time a Shuttle payload was managed from Florida. Two crew members also performed a spacewalk that lasted 7 hours, 5 minutes, and 28 seconds. It was the last in a series of generic spacewalks begun earlier in the year.

STS-58 (58th Shuttle flight)
18 October–1 November 1993
Columbia (15th flight)
Crew: John E. Blaha (Cdr), Richard A. Searfoss (Pilot),
Margaret R. Seddon (PC-MS1), William S.
McArthur, Jr. (MS2), David A. Wolf (MS3),
Shannon W. Lucid (MS4), Martin J. Fettman
(PS1)

STS-58 was the second dedicated Spacelab Life Sciences (SLS-2) mission. Fourteen experiments were conducted in fields such as regulatory physiology, cardiovascular/cardiopulmonary science, musculoskeletal science, and neuroscience. Eight of the experiments centered on the crew and six focused on 48 rodents carried on board. With the completion of her fourth spaceflight, Shannon Lucid accumulated the most flight time for a female astronaut on the Shuttle: 838 hours.

STS-61 (59th Shuttle flight)
2–13 December 1993
Endeavour (Fifth flight)
Crew: Richard O. Covey (Cdr); Kenneth D.
Bowersox (Pilot); Kathryn C. Thornton (MS1);
Claude Nicollier (MS2), ESA (Switzerland);
Jeffrey A. Hoffman (MS3); F. Story Musgrave
(PC-MS4); Thomas D. Akers (MS5)

This Shuttle flight was one of the most challenging and complex missions ever attempted. During a record five back-to-back spacewalks, totaling 35 hours and 28 minutes, two teams of astronauts completed the first servicing of the Hubble Space Telescope and installed technologies that corrected the spherical aberration manufacturing error of the Hubble. On the first spacewalk, which lasted 7 hours and 54 minutes, the two-person team replaced two Rate Sensor Units, two Electronic Control Units, and eight electrical fuse plugs. On the second spacewalk, which lasted 6 hours and 35 minutes, two astronauts installed new solar arrays. On the third spacewalk, the Wide Field/Planetary Camera (WF/PC) was replaced in about 40 minutes rather than in the 4 hours that had been anticipated. The same team of

The Peru-Bolivia border, part of the Amazon Basin, and the SLS-2 Laboratory Module as seen during STS-58. (STS058-76-041)

Story Musgrave performs repairs on the Hubble Space Telescope during STS-61. (STS061-104-007)

astronauts also installed two new magnetometers at the top of the telescope. On the fourth spacewalk, crew members removed and replaced the High-Speed Photometer with the Corrective Optics Space Telescope Axial Replacement unit. During this 6-hour-and-50-minute EVA, astronaut Thomas Akers set a new U.S. spacewalking record of 29 hours and 14 minutes. The final spacewalk replaced the Solar Array Drive Electronics unit and installed the Goddard High Resolution Spectrograph Redundancy kit and also two protective covers over the original magnetometers.

STS-60 (60th Shuttle flight)
3–11 February 1994
Discovery (18th flight)
Crew: Charles F. Bolden, Jr. (Cdr); Kenneth S. Reightler, Jr. (Pilot); N. Jan Davis (MS1); Ronald M. Sega (MS2); Franklin R. Chang-Diaz (MS3); Sergei K. Krikalev (MS4), RSA (Russia)

This first Shuttle flight of 1994 marked the first flight of a Russian cosmonaut on the U.S. Space Shuttle, which was part of an international agreement on human spaceflight. The mission also was the second flight of the SPACEHAB pressurized module and marked the 100th Get-Away Special payload to fly in space. Also on this mission, Discovery carried the Wake Shield Facility (WSF) to generate new semiconductor films for advanced electronics.

STS-62 (61st Shuttle flight)
4–18 March 1994
Columbia (16th flight)
Crew: John H. Casper (Cdr), Andrew M. Allen (Pilot), Pierre J. Thuot (MS1), Charles D. "Sam" Gemar (MS2), Marsha S. Ivins (MS3)

The primary payloads for this mission were the U.S. Microgravity Payload-2 (USMP-2) and the Office of Aeronautics and Space Technology-2 (OAST-2). USMP-2 included five experiments investigating materials processing and crystal growth in microgravity. OAST-2's six experiments focused on space technology and spaceflight. Both payloads were located in the payload bay, activated by crew members, and operated by teams on the ground.

STS-59 (62nd Shuttle flight)
9–20 April 1994
Endeavour (Sixth flight)
Crew: Sidney M. Gutierrez (Cdr), Kevin P. Chilton (Pilot), Jerome "Jay" Apt (MS1), Michael R. Clifford (MS2), Linda M. Godwin (PC-MS3), Thomas D. Jones (MS4)

The Space Radar Laboratory-1 (SRL-1) was the primary payload for this mission. It gathered data about Earth and the effect of humans on its carbon, water, and energy cycles. It was located in the payload bay, activated by crew members, and operated by teams on the ground. The German Space Agency (DARA) and the Italian Space Agency (ASI) provided one instrument, the X-band Synthetic Aperture Radar (X-SAR). This instrument imaged more than 400 sites and covered approximately

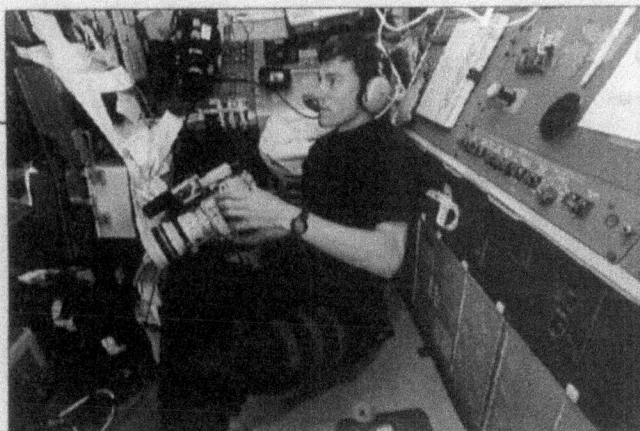
Cosmonaut Sergei Krikalev uses SAREX gear to talk to schoolchildren during STS-60. (STS060-29-009)

Aboard Space Shuttle Columbia (STS-62), mission commander John Casper (right) and mission specialist Sam Gemar prepare to take pictures of their home planet. (STS062-06-030)

38.5 million square miles (61.9 million square kilometers) of Earth.

STS-65 (63rd Shuttle flight)
8–23 July 1994
Columbia (17th flight)
Crew: Robert D. Cabana (Cdr); James D. Halsell, Jr. (Pilot); Richard J. Hieb (PC-MS1); Carl E. Walz (MS2); Leroy Chiao (MS3); Donald A. Thomas (MS4); Chiaki H. Naito-Mukai (PS1), NASDA (Japan)

STS-65 was *Columbia*'s last mission before its scheduled modification and refurbishment. This flight saw the first Japanese woman fly in space—payload specialist Chiaki Naito-Mukai. She also set the record for the longest flight to date by a female astronaut. The International Microgravity Laboratory flew for the second time, carrying more than twice the number of experiments and facilities as on its first mission. Crew members split into two teams to perform around-the-clock research on the behavior of materials and life in near weightlessness. More than 80 experiments, representing more than 200 scientists from six space agencies, were located in the Spacelab module in the payload bay. This flight also marked the first time that liftoff and reentry were captured on videotape from the crew cabin. This flight was the longest Shuttle flight to date, lasting 14 days and 18 hours.

STS-64 (64th Shuttle flight)
9–20 September 1994
Discovery (19th flight)
Crew: Richard N. Richards (Cdr), L. Blaine Hammond, Jr. (Pilot), Jerry M. Linenger (MS1), Susan J. Helms (MS2), Carl J. Meade (MS3), Mark C. Lee (MS4)

STS-64 marked the first flight of the Lidar In-Space Technology Experiment (LITE), which was used to perform atmospheric research. It also included the first untethered U.S. EVA in 10 years. LITE involved the first use of lasers for environmental research. During the mission, the crew also released and retrieved the SPARTAN-201 using the Remote Manipulator System arm.

STS-68 (65th Shuttle flight)
30 September–11 October 1994
Endeavour (Seventh flight)
Crew: Michael A. Baker (Cdr), Terrence W. Wilcutt (Pilot), Steven L. Smith (MS1), Daniel W. Bursch (MS2), Peter J. K. "Jeff" Wisoff (MS3), Thomas D. Jones (PC-MS4)

This mission marked the second 1994 flight of the Space Radar Laboratory (SRL-2), part of NASA's Mission to Planet Earth. Flying the SRL in different seasons allowed investigators to compare observations between the two flights. The mission also tested the ability of SRL-2 imaging radar to distinguish between changes caused by human-induced phenomena such as oil spills and naturally occurring events. Five Get-Away Specials were among the other cargo bay payloads. These included two by the U.S. Postal Service that held 500,000 commemorative stamps honoring the 25th anniversary of Apollo 11. STS-68 set another duration record, lasting more than 16.5 days.

Donald Thomas (left) and Robert Cabana (right) pose in front of *Columbia* following STS-65. (STS065(S)068)

This thermal tile damage to one of the pods protecting Space Shuttle *Endeavour*'s Orbital Maneuvering System occurred during STS-68. (STS068-067-013)

STS-66 (66th Shuttle flight)
3–14 November 1994
Atlantis (13th flight)
Crew: Donald R. McMonagle (Cdr); Curtis L.
Brown, Jr. (Pilot); Ellen Ochoa (PC-MS1);
Joseph R. Tanner (MS2); Jean-François
Clervoy (MS3), ESA (France); Scott E.
Parazynski (MS4)

STS-66 advanced data collection about the Sun's energy output, as well as the chemical makeup of Earth's middle atmosphere and how these factors affect global ozone levels, with the third flight of its Atmospheric Laboratory for Applications and Science (ATLAS-3). The other primary payloads were Cryogenic Infrared Spectrometers and Telescopes for the Atmosphere-Shuttle Pallet Satellite (CRISTA-SPAS), which continued the joint NASA-German Space Agency series of scientific missions, and the Shuttle Solar Backscatter Ultraviolet spectrometer (SSBUV). CRISTA-SPAS was released and retrieved using the Remote Manipulator System arm.

STS-63 (67th Shuttle flight)
3–11 February 1995
Discovery (20th flight)
Crew: James D. Wetherbee (Cdr); Eileen M. Collins
(Pilot); Bernard A. Harris, Jr. (PC-MS1); C. Michael
Foale (MS2); Janice E. Voss (MS3); Vladimir G.
Titov (MS4), RSA (Russia)

This mission had special importance as a precursor and dress rehearsal for the series of missions that would rendezvous and dock with the Russian space station *Mir*.

Discovery approached within 12.2 meters (40 feet) of *Mir*, then backed off to about 122 meters (400 feet) and performed a flyaround. The six-person crew included the second Russian cosmonaut to fly on the Space Shuttle. The mission also deployed the SPARTAN-204, a free-flying spacecraft that made astronomical observations in the far ultraviolet spectrum. The mission also included the third operation of the commercially developed SPACEHAB module, with its array of technological, biological, and other scientific experiments. Two crew members performed a spacewalk to test spacesuit modifications and demonstrate large-object handling techniques. On this mission, Eileen Collins became the first female Shuttle pilot and Bernard Harris became the first African American to walk in space.

STS-67 (68th Shuttle flight)
2–18 March 1995
Endeavour (Eighth flight)
Crew: Stephen S. Oswald (Cdr), William G. Gregory
(Pilot), John M. Grunsfeld (MS1), Wendy B.
Lawrence (MS2), Tamara E. Jernigan (PC-MS3),
Samuel T. Durrance (PS1), Ronald A. Parise
(PS2)

ASTRO-2 was the primary payload to fly on this mission. Its objective was to obtain scientific data on astronomical objects in the ultraviolet region of the spectrum. Its three telescopes made observations in complementary regions of the spectrum and gathered data that would add to scientists' understanding of the universe's history and the origins of stars. STS-67 set a new mission-duration record of 16.5 days.

ATLAS-3 payload in the cargo bay of *Atlantis*, seen in orbit during STS-66. (STS066-129-005)

Astronaut Bernard Harris checks the response of astronaut Janice Voss's muscles to microgravity during STS-63. (STS063-86-016)

STS-71 (69th Shuttle flight)
27 June 27–7 July 1995
Atlantis (14th flight)
Crew: Robert L. "Hoot" Gibson (Cdr); Charles J.
    Precourt (Pilot); Ellen Baker (–Shulman)
    (PC-MS1); Gregory J. Harbaugh (MS2);
    Bonnie J. Dunbar (MS3); Anatoly Y. Solovyev,
    Mir-19 (Cdr), up, Russia; Nikolai M. Budarin,
    RSC Energia (Russia), *Mir*-19 (flight engineer),
    up; Vladimir N. Dezhurov, *Mir*-18 (Cdr), down;
    Gennady M. Strekalov, RSC Energia (Russia),
    Mir-18 (flight engineer); Norman E. Thagard,
    Soyuz TM-21 (researcher), down

This flight marked the 100th U.S. human spaceflight and
was the first of a series of flights that docked with the
Russian space station *Mir*. On STS-71, *Atlantis* and *Mir*
remained docked for five days. The seven-person Shuttle
crew included two Russian cosmonauts who remained
on *Mir* after *Atlantis* returned to Earth. Two other cosmonauts and the U.S. astronaut Norman Thagard, who had
flown to *Mir* aboard the Russian *Soyuz* spacecraft in March
1995, returned to Earth on *Atlantis*. The mission demonstrated the successful operation of the Russian-designed
docking system, which was based on the concepts used in
the Apollo-*Soyuz* test program flown in 1975.

STS-70 (70th Shuttle flight)
13–22 July 1995
Discovery (21st flight)
Crew: Terence T. "Tom" Henricks (Cdr), Kevin R.
    Kregel (Pilot), Nancy J. Currie (formerly
    Sherlock) (MS1), Donald A. Thomas (MS2),
    Mary E. Weber (MS3)

The deployment of the Tracking and Data Relay Satellite
(TDRS-7) marked the completion of NASA's TDRS
system that provided communication, tracking, telemetry,
data acquisition, and command services to the Shuttle and
other low-orbital spacecraft missions. STS-70 also marked
the first flight of the new Block I Space Shuttle Main
Engine (SSME). The engine featured improvements that
increased the stability and safety of the main engines.

STS-69 (71st Shuttle flight)
7–18 September 1995
Endeavour (Ninth flight)
Crew: David M. Walker (Cdr), Kenneth D. Cockrell
    (Pilot), James S. Voss (PC-MS1), James H.
    Newman (MS2), Michael L. Gernhardt (MS3)

STS-69 deployed the Wake Shield Facility, which, flying
separately from the Shuttle, produced an "ultra vacuum" in
its wake and allowed experimentation in the production of
advanced, thin film semiconductor materials. The SPARTAN
spacecraft also was deployed and retrieved. The spacewalk on
this mission was the 30th Shuttle extravehicular activity.

STS-73 (72nd Shuttle flight)
20 October–5 November 1995
Columbia (18th flight)
Crew: Kenneth D. Bowersox (Cdr); Kent V. Rominger
    (Pilot); Kathryn C. Thornton (PC); Catherine G.
    "Cady" Coleman (MS1); Michael E. Lopez-
    Alegria (MS2); Fred W. Leslie (PS1); Albert
    Sacco, Jr. (PS2)

The second United States Microgravity Laboratory
(USML-2) was the primary payload on STS-73. Some of

Atlantis is shown docked with *Mir* during STS-71's visit to the Russian space station. (STS071-S-072)

Payload specialist Albert Sacco, Jr., inspects a crystal in a cylindrical autoclave on the middeck of the Earth-orbiting Space
Shuttle *Columbia*, mission STS-73. (STS073-353-018)

the experiments on USML-2 resulted from the outcome of investigations on the first USML mission that flew aboard *Columbia* on STS-50.

STS-74 (73rd Shuttle flight)
12–20 November 1995
Atlantis (15th flight)
Crew: Kenneth D. Cameron (Cdr); James D. Halsell, Jr. (Pilot); Chris A. Hadfield (MS1), CSA (Canada); Jerry L. Ross (MS2); William S. McArthur, Jr. (MS3)

STS-74 was the second in a series of *Mir* linkups. The mission delivered the Russian Docking Module to *Mir*, and it was attached permanently to the Kristall module, which gave better clearance for future Shuttle-*Mir* dockings. It also marked the first time that astronauts from the European Space Agency, Canada, Russia, and the United States were in space on the same complex at one time.

STS-72 (74th Shuttle flight)
11–20 January 1996
Endeavour (10th flight)
Crew: Brian K. Duffy (Cdr); Brent W. Jett, Jr. (Pilot); Leroy Chiao (MS1); Winston E. Scott (MS2); Daniel T. Barry (MS3); Koicho Wakata (MS4), NASDA (Japan)

The crew of STS-72 captured and returned to Earth a Japanese microgravity research spacecraft, the Space Flyer Unit (SFU), which had been launched by Japan in March 1995. The mission also deployed and retrieved the OAST-Flyer spacecraft, the seventh in a series of missions aboard reusable free-flying SPARTAN carriers. The flight

also included two spacewalks by three astronauts to test hardware and tools that will be used in the assembly of the International Space Station.

STS-75 (75th Shuttle flight)
22 February–9 March 1996
Columbia (19th flight)
Crew: Andrew M. Allen (Cdr); Scott J. Horowitz (Pilot); Franklin R. Chang-Diaz (PC); Jeffrey A. Hoffman (MS1); Maurizio Cheli (MS2), ESA (Italy); Claude Nicollier (MS3), ESA (Switzerland); Umberto Guidoni (PS1), ASI (Italy)

This mission was the 75th Shuttle flight and 50th Shuttle flight since NASA's return to flight following the *Challenger* accident. Its mission was a reflight of the Tethered Satellite System. The tether broke three days into the mission.

STS-76 (76th Shuttle flight)
22–31 March 1996
Atlantis (16th flight)
Crew: Kevin P. Chilton (Cdr); Richard A. Searfoss (Pilot); Ronald M. Sega (PC-MS1); Michael R. Clifford (MS2); Linda M. Godwin (MS3); Shannon W. Lucid (MS4), up

This mission featured the third docking between the Space Shuttle *Atlantis* and the Russian space station *Mir*. It included a spacewalk, logistics operations, and scientific research. More than 862 kilograms (1,896.4 pounds) of equipment were transferred from *Atlantis* to *Mir*, including a gyrodyne, transformer, batteries, food, water, film,

The Russian-built Docking Module (DM) sits in the back of *Atlantis*'s payload bay. It was attached to *Mir* during STS-74. (KSC-95EC-1616)

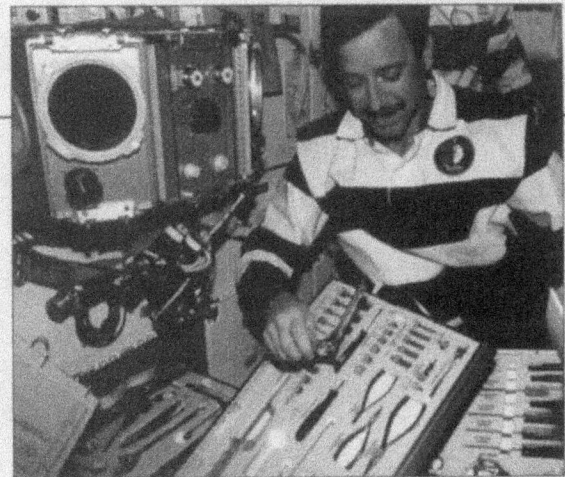

Pilot Scott Horowitz looks over tools he may use to perform an Inflight Maintenance (IFM) chore on the middeck of the Earth-orbiting Space Shuttle *Columbia* during STS-75. (STS075-333-032)

and clothing. Astronaut Shannon Lucid was the second American astronaut to stay on *Mir* and the first female American astronaut to fly to the station. This flight was the beginning of what would turn out to be Lucid's marathon stay aboard the space station.

STS-77 (77th Shuttle flight)
19–29 May 1996
Endeavour (11th flight)
Crew: John H. Casper (Cdr); Curtis L. Brown, Jr. (Pilot); Andrew S. W. Thomas (MS1); Daniel W. Bursch (MS2); Mario Runco, Jr. (MS3); Marc Garneau (MS4), CSA (Canada)

During this flight, the six-person *Endeavour* crew performed microgravity research aboard the commercially owned and operated SPACEHAB module. The crew also deployed and retrieved the SPARTAN-207 Inflatable Antenna Experiment (SPARTAN-IAE) satellite. A suite of four technology experiments called the Technology Experiments for Advancing Mission in Space (TEAMS) also flew in the Shuttle's payload bay.

STS-78 (78th Shuttle flight)
20 June 20–7 July 1996
Columbia (20th flight)
Crew: Terence T. "Tom" Henricks (Cdr); Kevin R. Kregel (Pilot); Richard M. Linnehan (MS1); Susan J. Helms (PC-MS2); Charles E. Brady, Jr. (MS3); Jean-Jacques Favier (PS1), CNES (France); Robert B. Thirsk (PS2), CSA (Canada)

The Life and Microgravity Spacelab (LMS) mission, building on previous Shuttle Spacelab flights dedicated to life sciences and microgravity investigations, studied the effects of long-duration spaceflight on human physiology and conducted the type of experiments that would fly on the International Space Station. The duration of this flight surpassed the longest Shuttle flight to date, lasting almost 17 days. Five space agencies participated in this mission.

STS-79 (79th Shuttle flight)
16–26 September 1996
Atlantis (17th flight)
Crew: William F. Readdy (Cdr); Terrence W. Wilcutt (Pilot); Jerome "Jay" Apt (MS1); Thomas D. Akers (MS2); Carl E. Walz (MS3); John E. Blaha (MS4), up; Shannon W. Lucid (MS4), down

On this mission, astronaut Shannon Lucid set the world's women's and the U.S. record for length of time in space: 188 days and 5 hours. The mission was the fourth Shuttle docking with the *Mir* space station. Astronaut Lucid returned to Earth on *Atlantis*, and astronaut John Blaha replaced her on *Mir*.

STS-80 (80th Shuttle flight)
19 November–7 December 1996
Columbia (21st flight)
Crew: Kenneth D. Cockrell (Cdr), Kent V. Rominger (Pilot), Tamara E. Jernigan (MS1), Thomas D. Jones (MS2); F. Story Musgrave (MS3)

STS-80 marked the third flight of the Wake Shield Facility (WSF) that flew on STS-60 and STS-69 and

This view of the Remote Manipulator System (RMS) end effector over an Earth limb with a solar starburst pattern behind it was taken during STS-77. (STS077-702-039)

Recovery convoy equipment greets *Columbia* following main gear touchdown on Runway 33 of Kennedy Space Center's Shuttle Landing Facility on 7 December 1996 (STS-80). (KSC-96EC-1339)

the third flight of the German-built ORFEUS-SPAS II. Both the WSF and the ORFEUS-SPAS were deployed and retrieved during the mission, making it the first time that two satellites were flying freely at the same time. The record for the longest Shuttle flight was broken again, with this flight lasting slightly more than 17.5 days.

STS-81 (81st Shuttle flight)
12–22 January 1997
Atlantis (18th flight)
Crew: Michael A. Baker (Cdr); Brent W. Jett, Jr. (Pilot); Peter J. K. "Jeff" Wisoff (MS1); John M. Grunsfeld (MS2); Marsha S. Ivins (MS3); Jerry M. Linenger (MS4), up; John E. Blaha (MS4), down

This mission was the fifth of nine planned missions to *Mir* and the second involving an exchange of U.S. astronauts. Astronaut Jerry Linenger replaced astronaut John Blaha aboard *Mir* after Blaha's 128 days in space. *Atlantis* carried the SPACEHAB double module, which provided additional middeck locker space for secondary experiments.

STS-82 (82nd Shuttle flight)
11–21 February 1997
Discovery (22nd flight)
Crew: Kenneth D. Bowersox (Cdr), Scott J. Horowitz (Pilot), Joseph R. Tanner (MS1), Steven A. Hawley (MS2), Gregory J. Harbaugh (MS3), Mark C. Lee (PC-MS4), Steven L. Smith (MS5)

STS-82 was the second in a series of planned servicing missions to the Hubble Space Telescope (HST). The orbiter's robot arm captured the HST so it could be serviced. In five spacewalks, the crew replaced the Goddard High Resolution Spectrograph and the Faint Object Spectrograph with the Space Telescope Imaging Spectrograph (STIS) and the Near Infrared Camera and Multi-Object Spectrometer (NICMOS). Crew members also replaced other hardware with upgrades and spares. HST received a refurbished Fine Guidance Sensor and a refurbished spare Reaction Wheel Assembly (RWA) to replace one of four RWAs. A Solid State Recorder replaced one reel-to-reel tape recorder. The crew members also replaced the HST's insulation, which had deteriorated due to rapid heating and cooling as the telescope moved into and out of sunlight and also due to constant exposure to the molecular oxygen encountered in the upper reaches of the atmosphere.

STS-83 (83rd Shuttle flight)
4–8 April 1997
Columbia (22nd flight)
Crew: James D. Halsell, Jr. (Cdr), Susan L. Still (Pilot), Janice E. Voss (MS1), Michael L. Gernhardt (MS2), Donald A. Thomas (MS3), Roger K. Crouch (PS1), Gregory T. Linteris (PS2)

This mission lasted only 4 days and returned to Earth 12 days early due to a problem with one of the fuel cells that provided electricity and water to the orbiter. The Microgravity Science Laboratory-1 (MSL-1) was rescheduled for a later mission.

Attached to the Remote Manipulator System, the Hubble Space Telescope is unberthed and lifted up into the sunlight during STS-82, the second servicing mission. (STS082-709-097)

Pilot Susan Still floats into the Spacelab Module in the early phases of its activation. Still, a member of the 1995 astronaut class, joined four other NASA astronauts and two scientist payload specialists for the Microgravity Science Laboratory 1 (MSL-1) mission aboard the Earth-orbiting Space Shuttle *Columbia*. (STS083-303-002)

STS-84 (84th Shuttle flight)
15–24 May 1997
Atlantis (19th flight)
Crew: Charles J. Precourt (Cdr); Eileen M. Collins
  (Pilot); Jean-François Clervoy (PC-MS1), ESA
  (France); Carlos I. Noriega (MS2); Edward T.
  Lu (MS3); Yelena V. Kondakova (MS4), RSC
  Energia (Russia); C. Michael Foale (MS5), up;
  Jerry M. Linenger (MS5), down

This was the sixth docking with the *Mir* space station
and the third involving an exchange of U.S. astronauts. Astronaut Mike Foale replaced astronaut Jerry
Linenger, who had been in space for 132 days. The
mission resupplied materials for experiments to be
performed aboard *Mir* and also returned experiment
samples and data to Earth.

STS-94 (85th Shuttle flight)
1–17 July 1997
Columbia (23rd flight)
Crew: James D. Halsell, Jr. (Cdr); Susan L. Still (Pilot);
  Janice E. Voss (MS1); Michael L. Gernhardt
  (MS2); Donald A. Thomas (MS3); Roger K.
  Crouch (PS1); Gregory T. Linteris (PS2)

The reflight of the Microgravity Science Laboratory
(MSL-1), which had flown on STS-83, took place on this
mission. (STS-83 was cut short due to fuel cell problems.)
The mission involved the same vehicle, crew, and experiment activities as planned on the earlier mission. MSL-1

focused on the phenomena associated with the routine
influence of gravity, including the behavior of materials
and liquids in a microgravity environment. The laboratory
was a collection of 19 microgravity experiments housed
inside a European Spacelab Long Module.

STS-85 (86th Shuttle flight)
7–19 August 1997
Discovery (23rd flight)
Crew: Curtis L. Brown, Jr. (Cdr); Kent V. Rominger
  (Pilot); Robert L. Curbeam (MS2); N. Jan Davis
  (PC-MS1); Stephen K. Robinson (MS3);
  Bjarni V. Tryggvason (PS1), CSA (Canada)

The primary payload for STS-85 was the second flight of
the Cryogenic Infrared Spectrometers and Telescopes for the
Atmosphere-Shuttle Pallet Satellite-2 (CRISTA-SPAS-2). It
was the fourth in a series of cooperative ventures between
the German Space Agency and NASA. CRISTA-SPAS-2
was deployed and retrieved using *Discovery*'s robot arm. Two
other instruments on board also studied Earth's atmosphere:
the Middle Atmosphere High Resolution Spectrograph
Instrument (MAHRSI) measured hydroxyl and nitric oxide,
while the Surface Effects Sample Monitor (SESAM) carried
state-of-the-art optical surfaces to study the impact of the
atomic oxygen and the space environment on materials and
services. The Technology Applications and Science (TAS-1),
the Manipulator Flight Demonstration, supplied by Japan,
and the international Extreme Ultraviolet Hitchhiker were
other mission payloads.

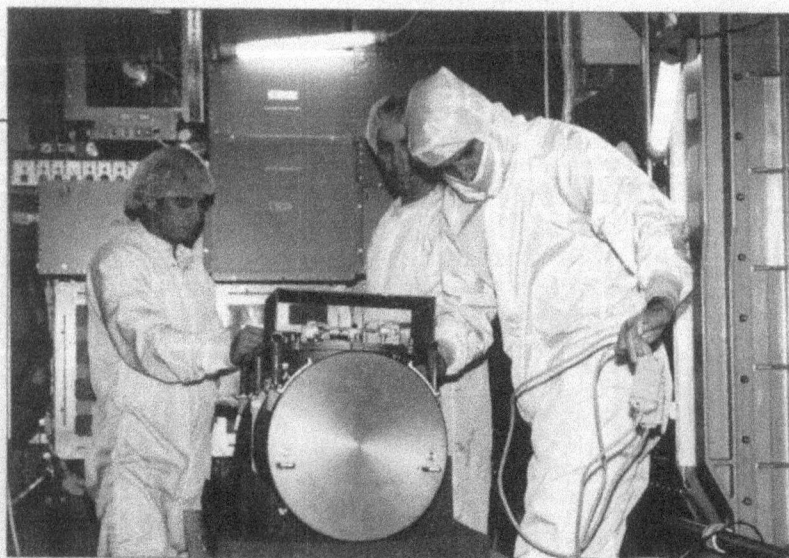

In the SPACEHAB Payload Processing Facility, McDonnell Douglas-SPACEHAB technicians prepare a Russian-made oxygen generator for flight in a SPACEHAB Double
Module. The oxygen generator was delivered to *Mir* during STS-84. (KSC-97PC-0676)

Space Shuttle orbiter *Discovery*'s payload bay doors are closed in preparation for the flight of mission STS-85.
(KSC-97PC-1130)

STS-86 (87th Shuttle flight)
25 September–6 October 1997
Atlantis (20th flight)
Crew: James D. Wetherbee (Cdr); Michael J.
Bloomfield (Pilot); Vladimir G. Titov (MS1),
RSA (Russia); Scott E. Parazynski (MS2);
Jean-Loup Chrétien (MS3), CNES (France);
Wendy B. Lawrence (MS4); David A. Wolf
(MS5), up; C. Michael Foale, down

This was the seventh docking between *Atlantis* and the Russian *Mir* space station and the fourth exchange of U.S. astronauts. The mission included a flyaround of *Mir* to determine the location of the puncture on the hull of the *Spektr* module. The *Mir* crew pumped air into the *Spektr* module, and the Shuttle crew observed that the leak seemed to be located at the base of damaged solar panel. U.S. astronaut Mike Foale returned aboard *Atlantis* after a stay of 134 days on *Mir*. His was the second longest single spaceflight in U.S. spaceflight history, behind Shannon Lucid's 188-day flight in 1996. *Atlantis* also carried the SPACEHAB double module to support the transfer of logistics and supplies for *Mir* and the return of experiment hardware and specimens to Earth.

STS-87 (88th Shuttle flight)
19 November–5 December 1997
Columbia (24th flight)
Crew: Kevin R. Kregel (Cdr); Steven W. Lindsey (Pilot);
Kalpana Chawla (MS1); Winston E. Scott (MS2);
Takao Doi (MS3), NASDA (Japan); Leonid K.
Kadenyuk (PS1), NSAU (Ukraine)

Experiments that studied how the weightless environment of space affected various physical processes and two spacewalks highlighted STS-87. During this mission, payload specialist Leonid Kadenyuk became the first Ukrainian to fly aboard the Space Shuttle. The mission was marked by an unexpected event when the attitude control system aboard the free-flying SPARTAN solar research satellite malfunctioned, causing the satellite to rotate outside the Shuttle. Crew members successfully recaptured the satellite and lowered it onto its berth in the payload bay. The capture took place during a spacewalk that lasted 7 hours and 43 minutes. A second spacewalk that lasted 7 hours and 33 minutes tested a crane to be used for constructing the International Space Station and a free-flying camera to monitor conditions outside the Station without requiring spacewalks.

STS-89 (89th Shuttle flight)
22–31 January 1998
Endeavour (12th flight)
Crew: Terrence W. Wilcutt (Cdr); Joe F. Edwards, Jr.
(Pilot); James F. Reilly (MS1); Michael P.
Anderson (MS2); Bonnie J. Dunbar (PC-MS3);
Salizhan S. Sharipov (MS4), RSA (Russia);
Andrew S. W. Thomas (MS5), up; David A.
Wolf (MS6), down

STS-89 featured the eighth *Mir*-Shuttle linkup and the fifth crew exchange. Astronaut David Wolf, who had been on *Mir* since September 1997, was replaced by astronaut Andrew Thomas.

The orbiter drag chute deploys after Space Shuttle *Atlantis* lands on runway 15 of the Kennedy Space Center Shuttle Landing Facility (SLF) after STS-86. (97PC-1492)

Columbia is lifted into high bay 3 in the Vehicle Assembly Building in preparation for STS-87. (KSC-97PC-1559)

STS-90 (90th Shuttle flight)
17 April–3 May 1998
Columbia (25th flight)
Crew: Richard A. Searfoss (Cdr); Scott D. Altman (Pilot); Richard M. Linnehan (MS1); Kathryn P. Hire (MS2); Dafydd R. Williams (MS3), CSA (Canada); Jay C. Buckey (PS1); James A. Pawelczyk (PS2)

STS-90 featured the 16th and final scheduled flight of the Spacelab science module in which *Columbia*'s astronauts conducted their research. Spacelab served as a science platform for Shuttle-based research over the previous 15 years. The key scientific aspects of the flight involved Neurolab, a set of investigations focusing on the effects of microgravity on the nervous system. Experiments studied the adaptation of the vestibular system and space adaptation syndrome, the adaptation of the central nervous system and the pathways that control the ability to sense location in the absence of gravity, and the effect of microgravity on a developing nervous system.

STS-91 (91st Shuttle flight)
2–12 June 1998
Discovery (24th flight)
Crew: Charles J. Precourt (Cdr); Dominic L. P. Gorie (Pilot); Franklin R. Chang-Diaz (MS1); Wendy B. Lawrence (MS2); Janet L. Kavandi (MS3); Valery V. Ryumin (MS4), RSC Energia (Russia); Andrew S. W. Thomas (MS5), down

STS-91 marked the ninth and final *Mir* docking for the Shuttle fleet, but the first for *Discovery*. Astronaut Andrew Thomas was brought back to Earth after a 130-day stay on the Russian station. This final mission to the *Mir* station marked the end of Phase 1 of the International Space Station (ISS). U.S. experiments present on the Station, including the Space Acceleration Measurement System (SAMS), the tissue engineering coculture (COCULT) investigations, two crystal growth experiments and eight Get-Away Special experiments, were transferred to SPACEHAB's single module. The Shuttle's robot arm's new electronics and software were tested in preparation for the construction of the ISS. STS-91 also marked the first mission to use the Super Lightweight External Tank, made of a new alloy combination that reduced the tank's weight by about 3,375 kilograms (7,425 pounds).

STS-95 (92nd Shuttle flight)
29 October–7 November 1998
Discovery (25th flight)
Crew: Curtis L. Brown, Jr. (Cdr); Steven W. Lindsey (Pilot); Stephen K. Robinson (MS1); Scott E. Parazynski (MS2); Pedro Duque (MS3), ESA (Spain); Chiaki H. Naito-Mukai (PS1), NASDA (Japan); John H. Glenn, Jr. (PS2)

The main objectives of the STS-95 mission were to deploy and retrieve the SPARTAN-201 free-flyer payload and conduct scientific experiments in the SPACEHAB module. In the payload bay, two experiments were carried out: the International Extreme Ultraviolet Hitchhiker payload and the Hubble Orbiting Systems Test (HOST). The scientific nature of the mission was overshadowed by the presence of John Glenn on the crew, flying again 36 years after becoming the first American to orbit Earth. President Bill Clinton was in attendance, marking the

James Pawelczyk, payload specialist, participates in a sensory motor and performance test on STS-90. Canadian astronaut Dafydd Williams is in the background. (STS090-349-019)

Backdropped against the darkness of space, Russia's *Mir* space station is captured on film as it moves away from Space Shuttle *Discovery* during the Shuttle-*Mir* final flyaround in June 1998. (STS091-711-028)

first time in Shuttle program history that a U.S. president attended a launch.

STS-88 (93rd Shuttle flight)
4–15 December 1998
Endeavour **(13th flight)**
Crew: Robert D. Cabana (Cdr); Frederick W. "Rick" Sturckow (Pilot); Jerry L. Ross (MS1); Nancy J. Currie (formerly Sherlock) (MS2); James H. Newman (MS3); Sergei K. Krikalev (MS4), RSA (Russia)

The STS-88 flight marked the first U.S. International Space Station (ISS) assembly flight, denoted 2A. The Remote Manipulator System arm grabbed the Unity (also known as Node 1) module from the Shuttle's cargo bay and connected it to the orbiter's docking system. Then, the robot arm grabbed the *Zarya* Control Module (also known as the Functional Cargo Block) and mated it to Unity. The *Zarya* module was launched on 20 November 1998 aboard a Russian Proton rocket. Three spacewalks were conducted by Jerry Ross and James Newman to attach cables, connectors and handrails between *Zarya* and Unity. The two astronauts also tested the Simplified Aid for EVA Rescue (SAFER) unit, a self-rescue device for spacewalkers who become separated from the spacecraft during EVA. Two satellites were also deployed, MightySat and SAC-A.

STS-96 (94th Shuttle flight)
27 May–6 June 1999
Discovery **(26th flight)**
Crew: Kent V. Rominger (Cdr); Rick D. Husband (Pilot); Tamara E. Jernigan (MS1); Ellen Ochoa (MS2); Daniel T. Barry (MS3); Julie Payette (MS4), CSA (Canada); Valery I. Tokarev (MS5), RSA (Russia)

STS-96 was the second ISS mission, denoted 2A.1, and marked the first Shuttle docking with the Station. *Discovery* docked to the Unity module, allowing the crew to enter the Station to perform maintenance and outfitting tasks. A spacewalk allowed Tamara Jernigan and Daniel Barry to install a U.S.-built crane and a Russian-built crane on the Station. Having been linked with the ISS for five days, *Discovery* undocked and performed a flyaround of the Station to obtain a detailed photographic record of the outpost. After the flyaround, the Starshine satellite was deployed from *Discovery*'s cargo bay.

STS-93 (95th Shuttle flight)
23–27 July 1999
Columbia **(26th flight)**
Crew: Eileen M. Collins (Cdr); Jeffrey S. Ashby (Pilot); Catherine G. "Cady" Coleman (MS1); Steven A. Hawley (MS2); Michel Tognini (MS3), CNES (France)

The objective of this mission, the shortest since 1990, was the deployment of the Chandra X-ray Observatory (previously known as Advanced X-ray Astronomy Facility [AXAF]). It was the third of NASA's Great Observatories. The deployment and two Inertial Upper Stage burns went as planned. Secondary scientific experiments occupied the crew for the rest of the mission.

The SPARTAN 201-05 is in the grasp of Space Shuttle *Discovery*'s Remote Manipulator System prior to release during STS-96. (STS095-E-5084)

The primary duty of the STS-93 crew was to deploy the Chandra X-ray Observatory, the world's most powerful x-ray telescope. (STS093-702-048)

STS-103 (96th Shuttle flight)
19–27 December 1999
Discovery (27th flight)
Crew: Curtis L. Brown, Jr. (Cdr); Scott J. Kelly (Pilot);
Steven L. Smith (MS1); Jean-Francois Clervoy
(MS2), ESA (France); John M. Grunsfeld
(MS3); C. Michael Foale (MS4); Claude
Nicollier (MS5), ESA (Switzerland)

This was the third mission to repair and upgrade the Hubble Space Telescope. After the telescope's capture by the robotic arm, it was placed on the Flight Support System in *Discovery*'s cargo bay. The repairs and upgrades were completed over the course of three spacewalks, performed by Steven Smith and John Grunsfeld, Mike Foale and Claude Nicollier, and again by Smith and Grunsfeld. During these spacewalks, the crew members changed and installed three new Rate Sensor Units (containing gyroscopes), six Voltage/Temperature Improvement Kits between the solar panels and the telescope's batteries, a computer, a fine guidance sensor, a transmitter, and a digital recorder.

STS-99 (97th Shuttle flight)
11–22 February 2000
Endeavour (14th flight)
Crew: Kevin R. Kregel (Cdr); Dominic L. P. Gorie
(Pilot); Gerhard P. J. Thiele (MS1), ESA
(Germany); Janet L. Kavandi (MS2); Janice E.
Voss (MS3); Mamoru M. Mohri (MS4),
NASDA (Japan)

STS-99's major payload was the Shuttle Radar Topography Mission. The orbiter's mast was deployed and the antenna was turned to its operation position so that mapping could begin 12 hours after launch. The mapping area covered a region ranging from 60 degrees north to 56 degrees south of the equator. Three crew members split into two shifts to operate 24 hours a day. The collected data, which approximated 20,000 CDs' worth, were sent to the Jet Propulsion Laboratory for analysis. A secondary payload was a student experiment, EarthKam, which took Earth photos trough one of *Endeavour*'s overhead flight-deck windows.

STS-101 (98th Shuttle flight)
19–29 May 2000
Atlantis (21st flight)
Crew: James D. Halsell, Jr. (Cdr); Scott J. Horowitz
(Pilot); Mary E. Weber (MS1); Jeffrey N.
Williams (MS2); James S. Voss (MS3); Susan J.
Helms (MS4); Yury V. Usachev (MS5), RSA
(Russia)

This mission was the third ISS flight, denoted 2A.2a. The mission consisted of one spacewalk, during which James Voss and Jeffrey Williams secured the U.S.-built crane, installed final parts of the Russian-built *Strela* crane, and replaced a faulty antenna. The Station was outfitted with different equipment outside during the spacewalk and inside after the Shuttle's crew opened the hatches between *Atlantis* and the Station. While inside the Station, the crew replaced or installed equipment consisting of batteries, smoke detectors, cooling fans, computer cables, a new communications memory unit and power distribution box, as well as supplies to support human activity aboard the Station. All items were stored in the SPACEHAB double module inside *Atlantis*'s cargo bay. STS-101 readied the Station for the arrival the of the

Astronaut John Grunsfeld, positioned on a foot retraint on the end of *Discovery*'s Remote Manipulator System (RMS), prepares to replace a radio transmitter in one of the Hubble Space Telescope's electronics bays on mission STS-103. (STS103-713-048)

Part of the Shuttle Radar Topography Mission (SRTM) hardware is seen here through *Endeavour*'s aft flight-deck windows about halfway through the scheduled 11-day SRTM flight on STS-99. The mast, only partially visible at lower right, is actually 60 meters (196.9 feet) in length. (S99-E-5476)

Zvezda Service Module, which launched 12 July 2000 on a Russian Proton rocket and docked two weeks later.

STS-106 (99th Shuttle flight)
8–20 September 2000
Atlantis (22nd flight)
Crew: Terrence W. Wilcutt (Cdr); Scott D. Altman (Pilot); Edward T. Lu (MS1); Richard A. Mastracchio (MS2); Daniel C. Burbank (MS3); Yuri I. Malenchenko (MS4), RSA (Russia); Boris V. Morukov (MS5), RSA (Russia)

STS-106 was the fourth flight to the ISS, denoted 2A.2b. A spacewalk performed by Edward Lu and Yuri Malenchenko involved routing and connecting power, data, and communications cables between the *Zvezda* and *Zarya* modules. The other objective of the spacewalk was to install a magnetometer, which serves as a compass. After the crew entered the ISS, more than three tons of hardware and supplies were transferred from the SPACEHAB double module to the Station in preparation for the outpost's first crew later in the fall.

STS-92 (100th Shuttle flight)
11–24 October 2000
Discovery (28th flight)
Crew: Brian K. Duffy (Cdr); Pamela A. Melroy (Pilot); Leroy Chiao (MS1); William S. McArthur, Jr. (MS2); Peter J. K. "Jeff" Wisoff (MS3); Michael E. Lopez-Alegria (MS4); Koicho Wakata (MS5), NASDA (Japan)

This mission was the fifth ISS flight, denoted 3A, and the third construction flight. The primary objectives were the installation of the Zenith 1 (Z1) truss and the third pressurized mating adapter (PMA3), which is used as a docking port. STS-92 also included four spacewalks. The first, by Leroy Chiao and William McArthur, involved connecting electrical umbilicals to provide power on the Z1 truss, relocating and deploying two antennas, and installing a toolbox for future on-orbit construction. The second spacewalk, made by Jeff Wisoff and Michael Lopez-Alegria, included the attachment of the PMA3 to the Station and preparation of the Z1 truss for installation of solar arrays planned for STS-97. The third spacewalk, performed by Chiao and McArthur, consisted of the installation of electrical converter units on the Z1 truss. The fourth and final spacewalk, by Wisoff and Lopez-Alegria, involved work on the Z1 truss. The final spacewalkers also tested SAFER. Equipment and supplies to support the first resident crew were transferred from *Discovery* to the Station.

STS-97 (101st Shuttle flight)
30 November–11 December 2000
Endeavour (15th flight)
Crew: Brent W. Jett, Jr. (Cdr); Michael J. Bloomfield (Pilot); Joseph R. Tanner (MS1); Marc Garneau (MS2), CSA (Canada); Carlos I. Noriega (MS3)

STS-97 was the sixth ISS flight, denoted 4A. Three spacewalks were performed by astronauts Joseph Tanner and Carlos Noriega, who accomplished the mating of the Port 6 (P6) truss and the first set of U.S.-provided solar arrays to the Station's Z1 truss, the preparation of the

Michael Lopez-Alegria works on the ISS during a long spacewalk as part of STS-92. (STS092-301-006)

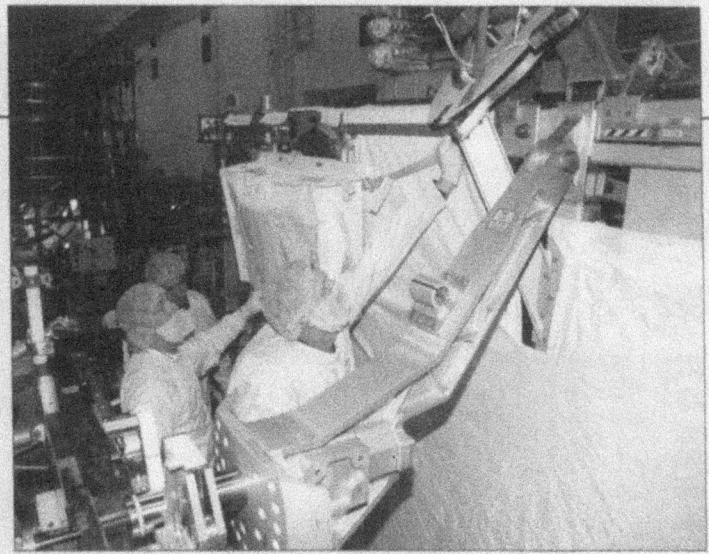

In the Space Station Processing Facility, STS-97 mission specialists Carlos Noriega (far left) and Joe Tanner (right) check out the mission payload, the P6 integrated truss segment. (KSC-00PP-1720)

Pressurized Mating Adapter 2 (PMA2) docking port, the installation of Floating Potential Probes (FPP) to measure electrical potential surrounding the Station, and the attachment of a camera cable outside the Unity module. On 8 December, hatches between *Endeavour* and the ISS were opened, allowing the transfer of supplies from the orbiter to the Expedition 1 crew aboard the Station.

STS-98 (102nd Shuttle flight)
7–20 February 2001
Atlantis (23rd flight)
Crew: Kenneth D. Cockrell (Cdr), Mark L. Polansky (Pilot), Robert L. Curbeam (MS1), Marsha S. Ivins (MS2), Thomas D. Jones (MS3)

STS-98 was the seventh ISS flight, denoted 5A. The purpose of the mission was to deliver, attach, and activate the U.S. Destiny laboratory module to the Station. Three spacewalks involved outfitting Destiny's exterior, moving the PMA2 from the Z1 truss to the Destiny module, and attaching a spare communications antenna to the Station. Mission specialists Robert Curbeam and Thomas Jones performed the three spacewalks in 19 hours and 49 minutes. Supplies were also delivered to the Station's crew.

STS-102 (103rd Shuttle flight)
8–21 March 2001
Discovery (29th flight)
Crew: James D. Wetherbee (Cdr), James M. Kelly (Pilot), Andrew S. W. Thomas (MS1), Paul W. Richards (MS2)

ISS Expedition 2 (launch): James S. Voss; Susan J. Helms; Yury V. Usachev, RSA (Russia)
ISS Expedition 1 (return): Sergei K. Krikalev, RSA (Russia); William M. Shepherd; Yuri P. Gidzenko, RSA (Russia)

STS-102 was the eighth ISS flight, denoted 5A.1. The flight's objectives were to replace the Expedition 1 crew and to unload supplies, equipment, and science racks from the first Multi-Purpose Logistics Module (MPLM). This Italian-built module, named Leonardo, was lifted from *Discovery*'s cargo bay and attached to the Unity module. This took place after a spacewalk by Susan Helms and James Voss was performed to make room on the Unity module for Leonardo. Astronauts placed the emptied module back in the Shuttle's cargo bay and returned it to Earth. A second spacewalk, by Paul Richards and Andrew Thomas that lasted 6 hours and 21 minutes, continued the outfitting of the Station through the installation of a coolant pump, an External Stowage Platform for spare Station parts, and connecting cables.

STS-100 (104th Shuttle flight)
19 April–1 May 2001
Endeavour (16th flight)
Crew: Kent V. Rominger (Cdr); Jeffrey S. Ashby (Pilot); Chris A. Hadfield (MS1), CSA (Canada); John L. Phillips (MS2); Scott E. Parazynski (MS3); Umberto Guidoni (MS4), ESA (Italy); Yuri V. Lonchakov (MS5), RSA (Russia)

In the Operations and Checkout Building, the U.S. Lab named Destiny reaches the open floor after being lifted out of the vacuum chamber where it was tested for leaks. During STS-98, the crew installed the Lab on the Space Station during a series of three spacewalks in February of 2001. (KSC-00PP-0870)

Astronaut Chris Hadfield, mission specialist representing the Canadian Space Agency, is seen near the Canadarm 2 as the new robotics tool for the ISS grasps the Spacelab pallet. Scott Parazynski participated in two days of extravehicular activity on the STS-100 mission. (STS100-342-010)

STS-100 was the ninth ISS flight, denoted 6A. The mission carried the Canadian-built Canadarm 2, which was attached outside the Station's Destiny module. Crew members also transferred supplies and scientific equipment racks to the Station via the second Multi-Purpose Logistics Module, named Raffaello. Scott Parazynsky and Chris Hadfield conducted two spacewalks to install an ultrahigh frequency (UHF) antenna to the Destiny module, connect cables between Canadarm 2 and Destiny, and continue the outfitting of the robot arm and Destiny. All of the mission's EVAs totaled 14 hours and 50 minutes.

STS-104 (105th Shuttle flight)
12–24 July 2001
Atlantis (24th flight)
Crew: Steven W. Lindsey (Cdr), Charles O. Hobaugh (Pilot), Michael L. Gernhardt (MS1), Janet L. Kavandi (MS2), James F. Reilly (MS3)

The 10th flight to the ISS was designated assembly flight 7A. The primary objective of the mission was to deliver the Quest Airlock, which allowed for spacewalks from the Station. The airlock was unloaded from *Atlantis*'s cargo bay and placed on the Unity node by Expedition 2 crew member Susan Helms. During this process, astronauts Michael Gernhardt and James Reilly provided guidance from outside the Station during their first of three planned spacewalks. The second spacewalk involved installing tank assemblies for the Joint Airlock. The third, during which the astronauts exited the ISS via the new airlock, consisted of installing another nitrogen tank to the airlock's shell. A total of four tanks were installed,

and their purpose is to pressurize the airlock and resupply spacesuits. Gerhardt and Reilly spent 16 hours and 30 minutes outside the Station.

STS-105 (106th Shuttle flight)
10–22 August 2001
Discovery (30th flight)
Crew: Scott J. Horowitz (Cdr), Frederick W. "Rick" Sturckow (Pilot), Patrick G. Forrester (MS1), Daniel T. Barry (MS2)
ISS Expedition 3 (launch): Frank L. Culbertson, Jr.; Vladimir N. Dezhurov, RSA (Russia); Mikhail V. Tyurin, RSA (Russia)
ISS Expedition 2 (return): Yury V. Usachev, RSA (Russia); James S. Voss; Susan J. Helms

Atlantis performed the 11th ISS flight, denoted 7A.1, whose main objective was to replace Expedition 2 crew members with Expedition 3 crew members. The mission also used Multi-Purpose Logistics Module (MPLM) Leonardo to unload 3,175.2 kilograms (7,000 pounds) of supplies, equipment, and science racks to the Station. Daniel Barry and Patrick Forrester completed two spacewalks, installing the Early Ammonia Servicer (EAS) and outfitting the Station in preparation for the arrival of the Starboard-Zero (S-Zero, S0) Integrated Truss Structure. Barry and Forrester spent a total of 11 hours and 45 minutes during EVAs. *Discovery*'s crew also deployed a small satellite, Simplesat, via a spring ejection system at the rear of the Shuttle's cargo bay.

STS-104, backdropped against the blue and white Earth some 237 miles below, the Quest Airlock is in the process of being installed onto the starboard side of Unity Node 1 of the ISS. Astronaut Susan Helms, Expedition 2 flight engineer, used controls on board the Station to maneuver the airlock into place with the Canadarm 2, or Space Station Remote Manipulator System. (STS104-E-5068)

View of Space Shuttle *Discovery* as it approaches the ISS during the STS-105 mission. Visible in the payload bay of *Discovery* are the MPLM Leonardo, which stores various supplies and experiments to be transferred into the ISS, and the Integrated Cargo Carrier (ICC), which carries the Early Ammonia Servicer and two Materials International Space Station Experiment (MISSE) containers. (ISS002-E-9749)

STS-108 (107th Shuttle flight)
5–17 December 2001
Endeavour (17th flight)
Crew: Dominic L. P. Gorie (Cdr), Mark E. Kelly
    (Pilot), Linda M. Godwin (MS1), Daniel M.
    Tani (MS2)
ISS Expedition 4 (launch): Yuriy I. Onufriyenko, RSA
    (Russia); Daniel W. Bursch; Carl E. Walz
ISS Expedition 3 (return): Frank L. Culbertson, Jr.;
    Vladimir N. Dezhurov, RSA (Russia); Mikhail
    V. Tyurin, RSA (Russia)

Endeavour completed the 12th ISS flight, denoted
Utilization Flight-1 (UF-1). STS-108 docked to the
Destiny module, hatches were opened, and the Station
crew exchanges took place. Aside from the crew swap,
the mission also moved Multi-Purpose Logistics Module
Raffaello, making its second spaceflight, from the Shuttle's
cargo bay to a docking port on the Unity module to allow
the transfer of 2,268 kilograms (5,000 pounds) of supplies
from Raffaello to the Station. One spacewalk, lasting 4
hours and 12 minutes, was performed by Linda Godwin
and Daniel Tanni to outfit the exterior of the Station.
Endeavour carried several Expedition 3 experiments back
to Earth, as well as experiments located inside *Endeavour's*
cargo bay. A small satellite, Starshine 2, was deployed
from a canister located in the cargo bay.

STS-109 (108th Shuttle flight)
1–12 March 2002
Columbia (27th flight)
Crew: Scott D. Altman, (Cdr), Duane G. Carey (Pilot),
    John M. Grunsfeld (MS1), Nancy J. Currie
    (formerly Sherlock) (MS2), Richard M.
    Linnehan (MS3), James H. Newman (MS4),
    Michael J. Massimino (MS5)

Although the mission was designated 3B, it was the fourth
Hubble Space Telescope servicing mission. John Grunsfeld,
Richard Linnehan, James Newman, and Michael
Massimino performed a record five spacewalks to upgrade
the telescope. The spacewalks, lasting 35 hours and 45
minutes, involved removal and installation of a new third-
generation solar array, the attachment of a new module to
dispense the power provided by the solar arrays, replacement of the original Faint Object Camera (FOC) with the
Advanced Camera for Survey (ACS), and the installation
a new experimental cooling system for the Near-Infrared
Camera and Multi-Object Spectrometer (NICMOS).

STS-110 (109th Shuttle flight)
8–19 April 2002
Atlantis (25th flight)
Crew: Michael J. Bloomfield (Cdr), Stephen N. Frick
    (Pilot), Rex J. Walheim (MS1), Ellen Ochoa
    (MS2), Lee M. E. Morin (MS3), Jerry L. Ross
    (MS4), Steven L. Smith (MS5)

The crew members of STS-106 pose for a traditional crew portrait on board the ISS. Front row, from left: Yuri Malenchenko, Terrence Wilcutt, and Scott Altman. Back row, from left: Daniel Burbank, Edward Lu, Richard Mastracchio, and Boris Morukov. (STS106-373-019)

This close-up view of the ISS, newly equipped with the 12,247-kilogram (27,000-pound) S0 truss, was photo- graphed by one of the astronauts on board Space Shuttle *Atlantis* during STS-110. S0 is the first segment of the Station's truss structure, which will ultimately expand the Station to the length of a football field. (STS110-729-055)

The 13th flight to the ISS was designated Station flight 8A. The main objective of the mission was to install the Starboard Zero (S0) truss and the Mobile Transporter, both of which were lifted out of *Atlantis*'s cargo bay and attached on top of the Destiny module. The truss contains navigational devices, computers, and cooling and power systems needed to attach additional laboratories to the outpost. The Mobile Transporter gives extra mobility to the Station's Canadarm 2. Rex Walheim, Steven Smith, Jerry Ross, and Lee Morin completed the installation of the S0 truss during four spacewalks totaling 28 hours and 22 minutes. In between spacewalks, astronauts also transferred oxygen and nitrogen, gases used to repressurize the module after spacewalks, to the Quest Airlock.

STS-111 (110th Shuttle flight)
5–19 June 2002
Endeavour (18th flight)
Crew: Kenneth D. Cockrell (Cdr); Paul S. Lockhart (Pilot); Franklin R. Chang-Diaz (MS1); Philippe Perrin (MS2), CNES (France)
ISS Expedition 5 (launch): Valery G. Korzun, RSA (Russia); Peggy Whitson; Sergei Y. Treschev, RSC Energia (Russia)
ISS Expedition 4 (return): Yuriy I. Onufriyenko, RSA (Russia); Daniel W. Bursch; Carl E. Walz

Endeavour completed the 14th flight to the ISS, named flight Utilization Flight-2 (UF-2). The Shuttle docked to the Destiny module, moved Multi-Purpose Logistics Module Leonardo from the Shuttle's cargo bay to the Unity module, and transferred more than 2,540 kilograms (5,600 pounds) of equipment, supplies, and experiments. The crew also moved the Mobile Remote Service Base System (MBS) from *Endeavour* to the Mobile Transporter on the Destiny lab. The MBS, part of the Station's Mobile Servicing System, will allow the Canadarm 2 to travel the length of the Station for construction tasks. Three spacewalks by Franklin Chang-Diaz and Phillipe Perrin, lasting 19 hours 31 minutes in total, continued the outfitting and maintenance of the Station. The astronauts replaced a wrist-roll joint on Canadarm 2, restoring it to full use. The mission also marked the arrival of Expedition 5, replacing Expedition 4, which returned to Earth aboard *Endeavour*.

STS-112 (111th Shuttle flight)
7–18 October 2002
Atlantis (26th flight)
Crew: Jeffrey S. Ashby (Cdr); Pamela A. Melroy (Pilot); David A. Wolf (MS1); Sandra H. Magnus (MS2); Piers J. Sellers (MS3); Fyodor N. Yurchikhin (MS4), RSC Energia (Russia)

STS-112, denoted ISS flight 9A, was the 15th flight to the Station and carried the S1 integrated truss segment and the Crew and Equipment Translation Aid (CETA) cart A to the Station. The CETA is the first of two human-powered carts to ride along the ISS railway, providing mobile work platforms for future spacewalking astronauts. Three spacewalks by David Wolf and Piers Sellers accomplished the installation of these primary payloads and spent 19 hours and 41 minutes performing these tasks.

STS-111 mission specialists Franklin Chang-Diaz (left) and, representing the French Space Agency (CNES), Philippe Perrin (right) work on the Mobile Remote Servicer Base System (MBS) on the ISS. (MSFC-0201905)

A view of the Starboard One (S1) truss, newly installed on the ISS, as photographed during the STS-112 mission's first scheduled session of extravehicular activity. (STS112-325-018)

STS-113 (112th Shuttle flight)
23 November–7 December 2002
Endeavour (19th flight)
Crew: James D. Wetherbee (Cdr), Paul S. Lockhart
(Pilot), Michael E. Lopez-Alegria (MS1), John B.
Herrington (MS2)
ISS Expedition 6 (launch): Kenneth D. Bowersox;
Nikolai M. Budarin, RSC Energia (Russia);
Donald Pettit
ISS Expedition 5 (return): Valery G. Korzun, RSA
(Russia); Peggy Whitson; Sergei Y. Treschev,
RSC Energia (Russia)

This 16th flight to the ISS, flight 11A, replaced the
Expedition 5 crew with Expedition 6 astronauts. Crew
members also lifted the Port 1 (P1) truss, stored in
Endeavour's cargo bay, with the Shuttle's robotic arm and
handed it to the Station's Canadarm 2, which placed it to
the installation position. Three spacewalks took place to
outfit and activate the truss. Michael Lopez-Alegria and
John Herrington performed the EVAs, which totaled 19
hours and 55 minutes.

STS-107 (113th Shuttle flight)
16 January–1 February 2003
Columbia (28th flight)
Crew: Rick D. Husband (Cdr); William C. McCool
(Pilot); Michael P. Anderson (PC); David M.
Brown (MS1); Kalpana Chawla (MS2); Laurel
B. S. Clark (MS3); Ilan Ramon (PS1), Israel

The first Shuttle flight of 2003 carried the first Israeli
crew member, Ilan Ramon. STS-107 was primarily a
microgravity and space science research mission, carrying aboard the SPACEHAB experiment module and a
number of external experiments. The mission included
the Freestar research payload, which consisted of several experiments. During reentry on 1 February, the
orbiter and crew were lost as *Columbia* broke apart
over central Texas. Sensors in the left main landing
gear wheel well first detected abnormally high temperatures, and similar readings spread throughout the
orbiter. Later investigation revealed that leading edge
wing tile was damaged by shed External Tank foam on
liftoff, and the compromised tile allowed superheated
gas to enter the orbiter during reentry.

STS-114 (114th Shuttle flight)
26 July–9 August 2005
Discovery (31st flight)
Crew: Eileen M. Collins (Cdr); James M. Kelly (Pilot);
Soichi Noguchi (MS1), JAXA (Japan); Stephen
K. Robinson (MS2); Andrew S. W. Thomas
(MS3); Wendy B. Lawrence (MS4); Charles J.
Camarda (MS5)

Discovery's flight marked the return to flight for the Shuttle
fleet, two and half years after the loss of *Columbia* and
its crew on mission STS-107, and the 17th flight to the
International Space Station, and was denoted Logistics
Flight 1 (LF1). During launch, *Discovery*'s condition was
extensively documented through a system of new and
upgraded ground-based cameras, radar systems, and air-
borne cameras aboard high-altitude aircraft. The imagery
captured of *Discovery*'s launch and additional imagery
from laser systems on *Discovery*'s new Orbiter Boom
Sensor System (OBSS), which is a 15.24-meter (50-foot)

Astronaut Michael Lopez-Alegria, STS-113 mission specialist, works on the newly installed P1 truss on the International Space Station dur-ing a session of extravehicular activity. (ISS005-E-21771)

The STS-107 crew members strike a "flying" pose for their traditional in-flight crew portrait in the SPACEHAB Research Double Module (RDM) aboard Space Shuttle *Columbia*. (STS107-735-032)

long boom extension of the Shuttle robotic arm laser-scanner, as well as data from sensors embedded in the Shuttle's wings helped determine the health of *Discovery's* thermal protection system. As *Discovery* approached the International Space Station, crew members aboard the Station photographed the orbiter's thermal protective tiles as well as areas around its main and nose landing gear doors. *Discovery's* commander also performed the first Rendezvous Pitch Maneuver. During the mission, Multi-Purpose Logistics Module Raffaello was lifted from *Discovery's* cargo bay for attachment to the Unity module by the Station's Canadarm 2, allowing the transfer of supplies and equipment to the station. Three thousand two hundred kilograms (7,055 pounds) of unneeded equipment and trash were transferred from the Station to the Raffaello module prior to its stowage inside *Discovery's* cargo bay. Three spacewalks were planned and performed by Stephen Robinson and Soichi Noguchi for a total of 20 hours and 5 minutes. During those spacewalks, the astronauts tested repair techniques on thermal tiles and reinforced carbon-carbon tiles; rerouted power to one the four Station gyroscopes; replaced another gyroscope with a new one; pulled the two protruding gap fillers from between thermal protection tiles; and, finally, installed a fifth Materials International Space Station Experiment (MISSE), which exposes samples of various materials to the harsh space environment for several months.

STS-121 (115th Shuttle flight)
4–17 July 2006
Discovery (32nd flight)
Crew: Steven W. Lindsey (Cdr); Mark E. Kelly (Pilot); Michael E. Fossum, (MS1); Lisa M. Nowak (MS2); Stephanie D. Wilson (MS3); Piers J. Sellers (MS4); Thomas Reiter (MS5), ISS (Flight Engineer), ESA (Germany), up

Discovery's flight marked the 18th ISS flight, denoted Utilization and Logistics Flight 1.1 (ULF 1.1). STS-121 carried on the analysis of safety improvements that debuted on the previous mission, STS-114, following the same inspection procedures carried on during that flight. *Discovery* carried the Italian-built Multi-Purpose Logistics Module Leonardo, which was moved from the Shuttle's cargo bay to the Unity module using the Station's Canadarm 2. Leonardo carried more than 3,357 kilograms (7,400 pounds) of supplies to the Station and brought back more than 2,086 kilograms (4,600 pounds) of experiments, unnecessary hardware, and trash to Earth. European Space Agency astronaut Thomas Reiter of Germany was delivered to the ISS as the newest member of ISS Expedition 13. The mission was extended one day, allowing time for an additional spacewalk. Piers Sellers and Michael Fossum performed three spacewalks in total, lasting 21 hours and 29 minutes total, to test the Shuttle's Remote Manipulator System/Orbiter Boom Sensor System (RMS/OBSS) combination as a platform for spacewalking astronauts, to perform maintenance on the Mobile Transporter, and to perform imagery and repair techniques to Reinforced Carbon-Carbon (RCC) tiles.

In the Space Station Processing Facility, the Control Moment Gyroscope (CMG), attached to the Small Adapter Plate Assembly, is lifted before being moved to the Lightweight Multi-Purpose Experiment Support Structure Carrier for flight. The CMG launched aboard Space Shuttle *Discovery* on Return to Flight mission STS-114. (KSC-05PD-0421)

STS-121 mission specialists Michael Fossum and Piers Sellers (out of frame) install the new trailing umbilical system in the mobile transporter on the International Space Station during the mission's second session of extravehicular activity. (S121-E-06211)

STS-115 (116th Shuttle flight)
9–21 September 2006
Atlantis (27th flight)
Crew: Brent W. Jett, Jr. (Cdr); Christopher J. Ferguson (Pilot); Joseph R. Tanner (MS1); Daniel C. Burbank (MS2); Heidemarie Stefanyshyn-Piper (MS3); Steven G. MacLean (MS4), CSA (Canada)

Atlantis's flight marked the 19th flight to the ISS, denoted flight ISS-12A. The orbiter delivered truss section P3/P4, a pair of solar arrays, and batteries, along with other supplies to the Station. During the course of three spacewalks, two by Joseph Tanner and Heidemarie Stefanyshyn-Piper and one by Dan Burbank and Steve MacLean (for a grand total of 20 hours and 19 minutes), the astronauts installed the newest structural and power generation component of the Station. The newly unfurled solar panels extended more than 35 meters (115 feet) in length, adding the power production capability for 60 kilowatts of electricity. The crew also conducted other maintenance work on the Station, preparing it for the next assembly mission.

STS-116 (117th Shuttle flight)
9–22 December 2006
Discovery (33rd flight)
Crew: Mark L. Polansky (Cdr); William A. Oefelein (Pilot); Nicholas J. M. Patrick (MS1); Robert L. Curbeam (MS2); Joan E. Higginbotham (MS4); Christer Fuglesang (MS3), ESA (Sweden); Sunita L. Williams (MS5), ISS (Flight Engineer), up; Thomas Reiter (MS5), ISS (Flight Engineer), ESA (Germany), down

This mission was the 20th ISS assembly flight, denoted 12A.1. STS-116 completed a major addition to ISS, adding the P5 truss segment and new solar arrays. *Discovery* also carried a SPACEHAB single logistics module in the cargo bay. This module contained 2,630 kilograms (5,800 pounds) of supplies and equipment that were transferred to the Station. In order to have enough clearance to deploy the new set of solar arrays, one of the power-generating arrays already on the Station and located on the P6 truss needed to fold up but failed to do so properly. Mission planners added a fourth spacewalk, which successfully corrected the malfunction. In addition to adding new Station components, the crew rewired the Station's power system to prepare for its final configuration. Three spacewalks were performed by Robert Curbeam and Christer Fuglesang and one was completed by Curbeam and Sunita Williams, for a total of 25 hours and 45 minutes spent outside the Station. Williams, who launched with STS-116, replaced Thomas Reiter as ISS flight engineer. Reiter, from Germany, returned with the crew aboard *Discovery*, which had its last mission before a major overhaul. STS-116 was the first mission to launch during the night since the *Columbia* accident, which previously resulted in stricter launch requirements (primarily for imagery purposes).

Astronaut Joe Tanner, STS-115 mission specialist, takes a break from the construction of the ISS to wave at the camera, held by Heidemarie Stefanyshyn-Piper. (S115-E-05753)

Against a black night sky, Space Shuttle *Discovery* and its seven-member crew head toward Earth orbit and a scheduled linkup with the International Space Station. (STS116-S-008)

THE INTERNATIONAL SPACE STATION

Overview

The International Space Station (ISS) represents the unprecedented cooperative efforts of 16 nations to undertake one of the largest and most complex scientific projects ever. The completed version of the ISS will be four times larger that the former Russian space station *Mir* and easily visible from Earth with the naked eye. Its massive interior space will be able to support a six-person crew that will conduct research and experiments that will help send humans back to the Moon, to Mars, and beyond.

The origins of ISS date back to the 1980s, when NASA drew up plans for an expandable station constructed of pressurized modules. President Ronald Reagan gave the proposal, then named Space Station *Freedom*, his seal of approval during the 1984 State of the Union Address. The program faltered in the following years, however, with numerous design changes and increasing cost outlooks. In the late 1980s, members of Congress threatened to kill the program, and in 1993, continued funding for the program was approved by a one-vote margin.

The original concept for the outpost included three separate orbital facilities—one crewed component and two platforms for experiments and planetary observation. The proposal would be a modular station that could be expanded as time went on and as needs required. Due to budget constraints, the design was continuously scaled back as the European Space Agency (ESA), Canada, and Japan agreed to collaborate with NASA on the project.

In 1994, a decade after Reagan's approval of the project, the Station received renewed interest from NASA, which reworked the design through the input of a number of private aerospace companies. President Bill Clinton also argued for increased international participation on the project, bringing the Russians firmly on board along with the members of the ESA, Canada, and Japan, resulting in the current ISS. Brazil was later brought into the program, expanding the number of members working to build a truly international space station. Clinton also saw that the final Station design would not include a modular expansion capability, thus limiting the Station's size and future budget requirements.

Russia launched the Functional Cargo Block (FGB), the first component of the ISS, in November 1998. The following month, the Space Shuttle *Endeavour* began assembly by adding Node 1, a core element of the Station that connects several different modules. The ISS was uninhabited until November 2000, when the first crew arrived at the Station aboard a Russian *Soyuz* vehicle. Expedition 1 included NASA astronaut William Shepherd and Russian cosmonauts Yuri Gidzenko and Sergei Krikalev, all of whom spent 136 days in orbit aboard the ISS.

While the Russian *Soyuz* and *Progress* vehicles made frequent resupply missions to the space-based outpost, the American Space Shuttle was established as the workhorse of the program. Not only are the Shuttle missions responsible for transporting the major components of the ISS into orbit, but they also carry the astronauts who actually put the massive modules, trusses, and solar arrays together more than 200 miles (321.8 kilometers) above Earth's surface. Following the initial assembly mission, STS missions

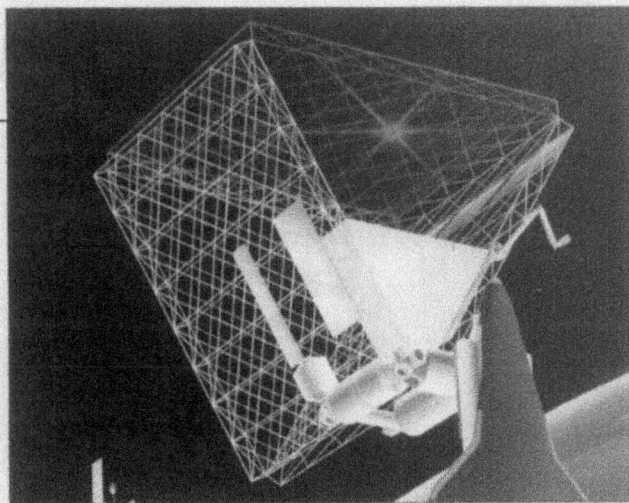

This is Johnson Space Center's 1984 "roof" concept for a space station. The "roof" was covered with solar array cells that were to generate about 120 kilowatts of electricity. Within the V-shaped beams there would be five modules for living, laboratory space, and external areas for instruments and other facilities. (84-HC-17)

MULTIMODULE OPERATIONAL NATIONAL MULTIPURPOSE SPACE STATION

This three-radial-module space station concept was intended to utilize Apollo hardware to deploy the station and to transfer crews to and from orbit. (GPN-2003-00103)

continued to put the ISS together with several flights in 2000, 2001, and 2002.

In February 2003, the program became jeopardized when STS-107 (*Columbia*) burned up while re-entering Earth's atmosphere, killing all seven crew members. As NASA worked to identify and correct the problem that caused the loss of *Columbia*, construction on the ISS came to a halt as the Shuttle fleet was grounded. The Station's crew was reduced to two and *Soyuz* and *Progress* became the only means of transporting passengers and supplies to the Station.

Shuttle flights resumed in July 2005 with the launch of STS-114. With the Space Shuttle program back on track by summer 2006, the crew complement was raised back to three and NASA picked up a regular construction schedule. The Shuttle's return to flight also brought with it another change: the Vision for Space Exploration. President George W. Bush unveiled this initiative in January 2004 following months of careful planning of America's new space policy direction. The plan calls for the completion of the ISS and the retirement of the Shuttle by 2010, followed by a human mission to the Moon by 2020 and an eventual crewed mission to Mars. With a little less than 50 percent of the Station completed in 2006, NASA plans an aggressive schedule to finish construction on time so that the outpost will be ready to support research for NASA's next missions.

When completed, the ISS will be the largest manufactured object to orbit Earth. It will have a mass of 419,580 kilograms (925,000 pounds), more than twice its mass of 185,976 kilograms (410,000 pounds) as of June 2006, and a length of about two and a half football fields. The final structure will run on only 110 kilowatts of power, which is less than the typical electrical output of a wind turbine with moderate winds.

Bibliography

NASA Sources

Kitmacher, Gary. *Reference Guide to the International Space Station* (NASA SP-2006-557). Available online at *http://www.nasa.gov/mission_pages/station/news/ISS_Reference_Guide.html*.

Web Links

NASA Station Home Page:
http://www.nasa.gov/mission_pages/station/main/index.html

Station Images and Videos:
http://spaceflight.nasa.gov/gallery/images/station/index.html

Non-NASA Sources

Hall, Rex (ed.). *The International Space Station: From Imagination to Reality*. British Interplanetary Society, London, 2002.

————. *The International Space Station: From Imagination to Reality, Volume 2*. British Interplanetary Society, London, 2005.

Harland, David, and John E. Catchpole. *Creating the International Space Station*. Springer-Praxis, 2002.

Launius, Roger D. *Space Stations: Base Camps to the Stars*. Smithsonian Books, Washington, 2003.

McCurdy, Howard E. *The Space Station Decision. Incremental Politics and Technological Choice* (New Series in NASA History). The Johns Hopkins University Press, Baltimore, 2000.

Crew portrait of the International Space Station (ISS) Expedition 1. From left to right are flight engineer Sergei Krikalev, commander Bill Shepherd, and *Soyuz* commander Yuri Gidzenko. (ISS01-S-002)

The ISS prepares for docking with *Atlantis* during the STS-104 mission while the Expedition 2 crew operates the Station. (STS104-E-5027)

International Space Station Expeditions

Expedition 1

31 October 2000–21 March 2001

Docking: 2 November 2000; Undocking: 18 March 2001

Launch aboard *Soyuz* TM-31, return aboard *Discovery* (STS-102)

Crew: William M. "Bill" Shepherd (ISS Cdr); Yuri P. Gidzenko (*Soyuz* Cdr), RSA (Russia); Sergei K. Krikalev (Flight Engineer), RSA (Russia)

Expedition 1 marked the first crew to inhabit the ISS. Upon docking with the *Zvezda* service module, the crew began setting up basic functions for the Station, including food preparation systems, sleeping quarters, and communication with mission controllers and NASA. In addition to conducting extensive press and documentary interviews, Expedition 1 also set up the computer systems required to run the Station. Along with logistical tasks, the crew also conducted experiments monitoring the environment of the ISS and investigating crew health and nutrition issues.

Expedition 2

8 March–22 August 2001

Docking: 10 March 2001; Undocking: 20 August 2001

Launch aboard *Discovery* (STS-102), return aboard *Discovery* (STS-105)

Crew: Yury V. Usachev (ISS Cdr), RSA (Russia); James S. Voss (Flight Engineer); Susan J. Helms (Flight Engineer)

Expedition 2 saw increased construction of the ISS during a series of four Space Shuttle missions and one *Soyuz*

mission to the outpost. During the crew's time in space, astronauts added the Space Station Remote Manipulator System (SSRMS), similar to the Space Shuttle's robotic arm. ISS crew members used the SSRMS to install a new airlock. The arm would be used on future missions to assist with the construction of the Station. Expedition 2 crew members also conducted an expanded number of science experiments compared to the previous crew, studying topics ranging from protein crystal growth to the ability of plants to survive in space.

Expedition 3

10 August–17 December 2001

Docking: 12 August 2001; Undocking: 15 December 2001

Launch aboard *Discovery* (STS-105), return aboard *Endeavour* (STS-108)

Crew: Frank L. Culbertson, Jr. (ISS Cdr); Vladimir N. Dezhurov (*Soyuz* Cdr), RSA (Russia); Mikhail V. Tyurin (Flight Engineer), RSA (Russia)

During the course of four spacewalks, the Expedition 3 crew continued with the on-orbit construction and maintenance of the ISS. Three spacewalks were dedicated to the installation of the *Pirs* Russian Docking Compartment, which allows the ISS to join with other spacecraft and provides egress for ISS crew spacewalks. One other extravehicular activity was dedicated to repairing an obstruction that prevented a *Progress* supply ship from mating with the Station. Expedition 3 was in space during the 11 September 2001 terrorist attacks, and crew members took photos of the devastation at the World Trade Center site.

Cosmonaut Vladimir Dezhurov, Expedition 3 flight engineer, floats in the pressurized adapter of the Functional Cargo Block on the International Space Station. (ISS003-E-6852)

Expedition 3 commander Frank Culbertson receives a haircut from Mikhail Tyurin in the *Zvezda* Service Module on the ISS. Culbertson is holding a vacuum device to collect the clippings. (ISS003-E-5896)

Expedition 4
5 December 2001–19 June 2002
Docking: 7 December 2001; Undocking: 15 June 2002
Launch aboard *Endeavour* (STS-108), return aboard
  Endeavour (STS-111)
Crew: Yuriy I. Onufriyenko (ISS Cdr), RSA (Russia);
  Daniel W. Bursch (Flight Engineer); Carl E.
  Walz (Flight Engineer)

During the fourth crew stay on the ISS, flight engineers Carl Walz and Dan Bursch broke the U.S. spaceflight endurance record of 188 days by spending 231 and then 227 total days in space. This record has since been broken. Expedition 4 saw the addition of one truss section, and each of the three crew members conducted spacewalks to perform modification and minor installation on the exterior of the ISS.

Expedition 5
5 June–7 December 2002
Docking: 7 June 2002; Undocking: 2 December 2002
Launch aboard *Endeavour* (STS-111), return aboard
  Endeavour (STS-113)
Crew: Valery G. Korzun (ISS Cdr), RSA (Russia);
  Peggy Whitson (Flight Engineer); Sergei Y.
  Treschev (Flight Engineer), RSC Energia
  (Russia)

Expedition 5 crew members inhabited the ISS during a time of relatively few additions to the Station—only two truss sections were installed. The crew conducted two spacewalks to install several minor components on the outside of the Station; however, they made up for a lull in construction with more than 30 experiments. Crew members conducted research projects to study latent virus shedding in space, zeolite crystal growth, and liver cell functions.

Expedition 6
23 November 2002–3 May 2003
Docking: 25 November 2002; Undocking: 3 May 2003
Launch aboard *Endeavour* (STS-113), return aboard
  Soyuz TMA-2
Crew: Kenneth D. Bowersox (ISS Cdr); Donald Pettit
  (Flight Engineer); Nikolai M. Budarin (Flight
  Engineer), RSC Energia (Russia)

During Expedition 6's time in space, *Columbia* broke apart during reentry, grounding all Shuttle missions and forcing the Station to rely on Russian vehicles. Despite the halt in the delivery of new Station components from the Space Shuttle, the crew conducted two spacewalks to outfit the exterior trusses and prepared them for future installation missions. Due to the inoperability of the Space Shuttle fleet, Expedition 6 returned aboard *Soyuz*, marking the first time that U.S. astronauts returned to Earth in that Russian vehicle.

Expedition 7
25 April–27 October 2003
Docking: 28 April 2003; Undocking: 27 October 2003
Launch and return aboard *Soyuz TMA-2*
Crew: Yuri I. Malenchenko (ISS Cdr), RSA (Russia);
  Edward T. Lu (Flight Engineer)

Expedition 7 marked the first two-person crew to inhabit the Station. This change resulted from the ongoing grounding of the Shuttle fleet and investigation into the *Columbia* accident. Yuri Malenchenko and Ed Lu also did not see anyone else during close to 200 days in space, until the arrival of

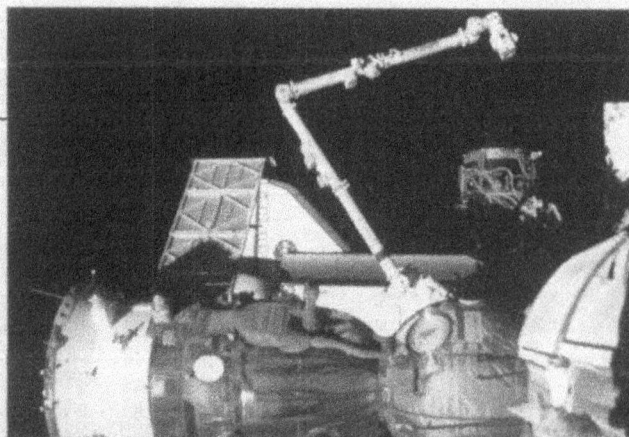

Moments prior to the undocking of Space Shuttle *Atlantis* from the ISS, an Expedition 4 crew member took this digital still photograph from a window in the *Pirs* Docking Compartment. Visible in this image are the *Soyuz* spacecraft, Space Station Remote Manipulator System (SSRMS)/Canadarm 2, and Pressurized Mating Adapter 3. (ISS004-E-10071)

The *Soyuz TMA-2* spacecraft, docked to the Functional Cargo Block's nadir port on the ISS, was photographed by an Expedition 7 crew member. The blackness of space and Earth's horizon provide the backdrop for the scene. (ISS007-E-05454)

Expedition 8. The crew became focused on Station operations and experiments and conducted no EVAs.

Expedition 8

18 October 2003–29 April 2004
Docking: 20 October 2003; Undocking: 29 April 2004
Launch and return aboard *Soyuz TMA-3*
Crew: C. Michael Foale (ISS Cdr); Alexander Y. Kaleri (Flight Engineer), RSC Energia (Russia); Pedro Duque (Flight Engineer; launched with Expedition 8 and returned with Expedition 7), ESA (Spain)

Expedition 8 launched with three crew members, though only two of them were actually headed to spend a significant amount of time on the Station. Spanish flight engineer Pedro Duque launched with Expedition 8 but returned with the Expedition 7 crew. This began a trend that continued until the Station crew complement returned to three. While aboard the ISS, Mike Foale and Alexander Kaleri continued to maintain the Station as the *Columbia* investigation continued. The crew's only spacewalk was cut short when Kaleri's Russian Orlan spacesuit malfunctioned.

Expedition 9

18 April–23 October 2004
Docking: 21 April 2004; Undocking: 23 October 2004
Launch and return aboard *Soyuz TMA-4*
Crew: Gennady I. Padalka (ISS Cdr), RSA (Russia;) E. Michael Fincke (Flight Engineer); André Kuipers (Flight Engineer; launched with Expedition 9 and returned with Expedition 8), ESA (the Netherlands)

With the Space Shuttle fleet still out of service, the crew of Expedition 9 continued to focus on Station operations and scientific research. The crew's first spacewalk ended early due to a pressure problem in Mike Fincke's suit, but was rescheduled. Gennady Padalka and Fincke conducted three additional EVAs, replacing exterior Station parts; preparing the Station for the arrival of the first ESA Automated Transfer Vehicle (ATV), to be launched on top of an Ariane 5 rocket; and installing additional communications antennas.

Expedition 10

13 October 2004–24 April 2005
Docking: 15 October 2004; Undocking: 24 April 2005
Launch and return aboard *Soyuz TMA-5*
Crew: Leroy Chiao (ISS Cdr); Salizhan S. Sharipov (Flight Engineer), RSA (Russia); Yuri G. Shargin (Flight Engineer; launched with Expedition 10, returned with Expedition 9), RSA (Russia)

Mission planners delayed the launch of the 10th crewed expedition to the ISS by five days after an explosive bolt on the *Soyuz* vehicle detonated during launch preparation. Following the delay, the mission ran smoothly, with the crew completing the installation of the Universal Work Platform outside the Station and installing navigational and communications equipment to facilitate the arrival of the first Automated Transfer Vehicle cargo ship. During the 2004 U.S. presidential election, Leroy Chiao became the first astronaut to vote in space, making his choice through an electronic ballot sent to the Station.

Two days after launching from Kazakhstan, the *Soyuz TMA-3* spacecraft, carrying the two Expedition 8 crew members, astronaut C. Michael Foale (American commander and NASA ISS science officer) and Russian cosmonaut Alexander Kaleri (flight engineer and *Soyuz* commander), along with European Space Agency astronaut Pedro Duque, docked with the International Space Station on 20 October 2003. (ISS007-E-17748)

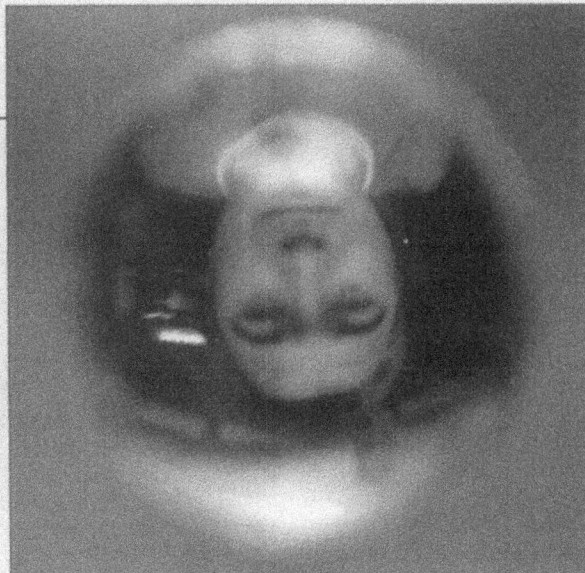

Salizhan Sharipov, Expedition 10 flight engineer, is reflected in a water bubble floating inside the ISS. (ISS010-E-13645)

Expedition 11
14 April–10 October 2005
Docking: 16 April 2005; Undocking: 10 October 2005
Launch and return aboard *Soyuz TMA-6*
Crew: Sergei K. Krikalev (ISS Cdr), RSA (Russia);
    John L. Phillips (Flight Engineer); Roberto
    Vittori (Flight Engineer; launched with
    Expedition 11, returned with Expedition 10),
    ESA (Italy)

Expedition 11 sent Sergei Krikalev, a space veteran, back to the Station for a second tour of duty. On 16 August 2005, Krikalev broke the previous 748-day record for most time spent in space by a human. The crew conducted one spacewalk, removing experiment containers, installing a television camera on the *Zvezda* Service Module, and removing two exterior panels. While the Space Shuttle returned to flight with STS-114 in late July, *Discovery* and its crew did not make a visit to the ISS.

Expedition 12
30 September 2005–8 April 2006
Docking: 3 October 2005; Undocking: 8 April 2006
Launch and return aboard *Soyuz TMA-7*
Crew: William S. "Bill" McArthur (ISS Cdr); Valery I.
    Tokarev (Flight Engineer), RSA (Russia)

Instead of the brief third crew member visit during two-person Station operations, American entrepreneur and space tourist Gregory Olsen joined the Expedition 12 crew as they launched to the Station aboard *Soyuz*. Olsen returned with the Expedition 11 crew after a brief stay aboard the ISS. Both Expedition 12 crew members par-

ticipated in two EVAs, installing a new camera, conducting minor repairs, and jettisoning an old Orlan spacesuit and a nonfunctional instrument.

Expedition 13
29 March–28 September 2006
Docking: 31 March 2006; Undocking: 28 September 2006
Launch and return aboard *Soyuz TMA-8*
Crew: Pavel V. Vinogradov (ISS Cdr), RSC Energia
    (Russia); Jeffrey N. Williams (Flight Engineer);
    Thomas Reiter (Flight Engineer; arrived at
    the ISS on 6 July 2006 aboard *Discovery* on
    STS-121), ESA (Germany); Marco Pontes
    (Flight Engineer; launched with Expedition 13,
    returned with Expedition 12), Brazilian Space
    Agency (Brazil)

Though launched with only two crew members, Expedition 13 received a third astronaut from STS-121, the first Shuttle mission to the ISS following the *Columbia* accident. Though the Station's crew complement was returned to three, *Discovery* did not deliver any new major components to the orbital outpost during its trip there. The 13th ISS crew conducted two spacewalks to conduct repairs and maintenance and the installation of an electric potential measurement device.

Expedition 14
18 September 2006–21 April 2007
Docking: 20 September 2006
Launch and return aboard *Soyuz TMA-9*

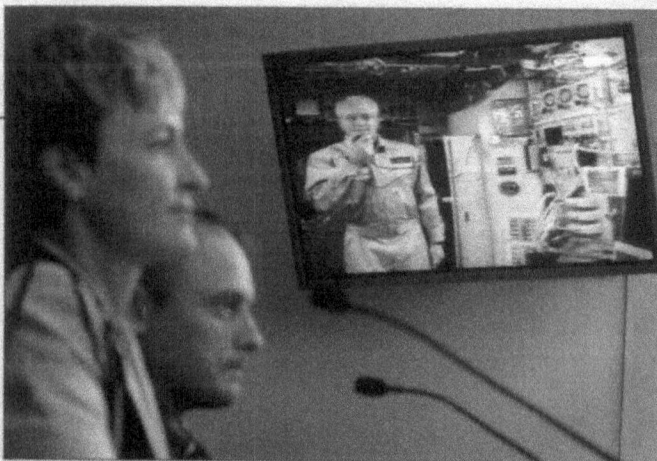

While orbiting Earth aboard the ISS at a speed of 5 miles a second, astronaut John Phillips, NASA ISS science officer and flight engineer on Expedition 11, testifies via video screen before the House Subcommittee on Space and Aeronautics, chaired by Representative Ken Calvert (R-California). (JSC2005-E-22365)

Expedition 13 science officer Jeffrey Williams floats outside the ISS during a spacewalk. (ISS013-E-63440)

Crew: Michael E. Lopez-Alegria (ISS Cdr); Mikhail
V. Tyurin (Flight Engineer), RSA (Russia);
Thomas Reiter (Flight Engineer; remained on
the Station from Expedition 13, returned on
Atlantis on STS-116 in December 2006), ESA
(Germany); Sunita L. Williams (Flight Engineer,
replaced Thomas Reiter after arriving on
STS-116, returned on *Atlantis* on STS-117)

Thomas Reiter remained on board the ISS for Expedition
14 and was joined by two additional crew members. A
second space tourist to ISS, American businesswoman
Anousheh Ansari, launched with Expedition 14 and
returned to Earth with the former crew. Expedition 14
crew members continued construction on the Station
with an operational Shuttle fleet. On Expedition 14's first
spacewalk, which involved installing experiments and
equipment, Mikhail Tyurin hit a golf ball from the *Pirs*
docking compartment.

Starboard side view of the International Space Station as it appeared
beginning 29 November 2004, represented by a computer-generated
scene. (JSC2004-E-51834)

An Expedition 13 crew member aboard the International Space Station
took this digital still image of Space Shuttle *Atlantis* as the Shuttle, carrying a crew of six, approached the orbital outpost. (ISS013-E-79714)

A *Soyuz* rocket launches from the Baikonur Cosmodrome,
Kazakhstan, with Expedition 12 commander William McArthur, Jr.,
flight engineer and *Soyuz* commander Valery Tokarev, and U.S.
spaceflight participant Gregory Olsen aboard. (jsc2005e40271)

APPENDIX A: SHUTTLE MAIN PAYLOADS

Shuttle Mission	Major Payloads	Shuttle Mission	Major Payloads
01. STS-1	N/A	36. STS-41	Ulysses; SSBUV; ISAC
02. STS-2	OSTA-1	37. STS-38	Department of Defense
03. STS-3	OSS-1	38. STS-35	ASTRO-1
04. STS-4	Department of Defense and CFES	39. STS-37	GRO
05. STS-5	Anik C-3; SBS-C	40. STS-39	Department of Defense: AFP-675; IBSS; SPAS-II
06. STS-6	TDRS-1	41. STS-40	SLS-1
07. STS-7	Anik C-2; Palapa B-1	42. STS-43	TDRS-E; SSBUV; SHARE-II
08. STS-8	Insat-1B	43. STS-48	UARS
09. STS-9	Spacelab-1	44. STS-44	Department of Defense: DSP
10. 41-B	Westar-VI; Palapa B2	45. STS-42	IML-1
11. 41-C	LDEF deploy	46. STS-45	ATLAS-1
12. 41-D	SBS-D; Syncom IV-2; TELSTAR	47. STS-49	Intelsat VI repair
13. 41-G	ERBS; OSTA-3	48. STS-50	USML-1
14. 51-A	TELESAT-H; Syncom IV-1	49. STS-46	TSS-1; EURECA deploy
15. 51-C	Department of Defense	50. STS-47	Spacelab-J
16. 51-D	TELESAT-I; Syncom IV-3	51. STS-52	USMP-1; LAGEOS II
17. 51-B	Spacelab-3	52. STS-53	Department of Defense; ODERACS
18. 51-G	MORELOS-A; ARABSAT-A; TELSTAR-3D	53. STS-54	TDRS-F; DXS
19. 51-F	Spacelab-2	54. STS-56	ATLAS-2; SPARTAN-201
20. 51-I	ASC-1; AUSSAT-1; Syncom IV-4	55. STS-55	Spacelab D-2
21. 51-J	Department of Defense	56. STS-57	SPACEHAB-1; EURECA retrieval
22. 61-A	Spacelab D-1	57. STS-51	ACTS/TOS; ORFEUS-SPAS
23. 61-B	MORELOS-B; AUSSAT-2; SATCOM KU-2	58. STS-58	SLS-2
24. 61-C	SATCOM KU-1	59. STS-61	First HST servicing
25. 51-L	TDRS-2; SPARTAN-203	60. STS-60	WSF-1; SPACEHAB-2
26. STS-26	TDRS-C	61. STS-62	USMP-2; OAST-2
27. STS-27	Department of Defense	62. STS-59	SRL-1
28. STS-29	TDRS-D	63. STS-65	IML-2
29. STS-30	Magellan	64. STS-64	LITE; SPARTAN-201
30. STS-28	Department of Defense	65. STS-68	SRL-2
31. STS-34	Galileo; SSBUV	66. STS-66	ATLAS-3; CRISTA-SPAS
32. STS-33	Department of Defense	67. STS-63	SPACEHAB-3; *Mir* rendezvous
33. STS-32	Syncom IV-F5; LDEF retrieval	68. STS-67	ASTRO-2
34. STS-36	Department of Defense	69. STS-71	First *Mir* docking
35. STS-31	HST deployment	70. STS-70	TDRS-G

Shuttle Mission	Major Payloads
71. STS-69	SPARTAN 201-03; WSF-2
72. STS-73	USML-2
73. STS-74	Second *Mir* docking
74. STS-72	SFU; OAST-Flyer
75. STS-75	TSS-1R; USMP-3
76. STS-76	Third *Mir* docking; SPACEHAB
77. STS-77	SPACEHAB; SPARTAN (IAE)
78. STS-78	LMS
79. STS-79	Fourth *Mir* docking; SPACEHAB
80. STS-80	ORFEUS-SPAS II; WSF-3
81. STS-81	Fifth *Mir* Docking; SPACEHAB
82. STS-82	Second HST servicing
83. STS-83	MSL-1
84. STS-84	Sixth *Mir* docking; SPACEHAB
85. STS-94	MSL-1 (reflight)
86. STS-85	CRISTA-SPAS
87. STS-86	Seventh *Mir* docking; SPACE-HAB
88. STS-87	USMP-4; Spartan; CUE
89. STS-89	Eighth *Mir* docking; SPACEHAB
90. STS-90	Neurolab
91. STS-91	Ninth and final *Mir* docking
95. STS-95	Spartan; HOST; John Glenn flight
93. STS-88	First ISS mission, 2A; Unity module
94. STS-96	Second ISS mission, 2A.1; Equipment
95. STS-93	Chandra X-ray Observatory
96. STS-103	Third HST servicing
97. STS-99	SRTM
98. STS-101	Third ISS mission, 2A.2a; Equipment
99. STS-106	Fourth ISS mission, 2A.2b; Magnetometer
100. STS-92	Fifth ISS mission, 3A; Z1 truss; PMA 3
101. STS-97	Sixth ISS mission, 4A; P6 truss

Shuttle Mission	Major Payloads
102. STS-98	Seventh ISS mission, 5A; U.S. lab Destiny
103. STS-102	Eighth ISS mission, 5A.1; MPLM Leonardo; Expedition 2 crew exchange
104. STS-100	Ninth ISS mission, 6A; Canadarm 2; MPLM Raffaello
105. STS-104	10th ISS mission, 7A; Quest Airlock; High-Pressure Gas Assembly
106. STS-105	11th ISS mission, 7A.1; MPLM Leonardo; Expedition 3 crew exchange
107. STS-108	12th ISS mission, UF-1; MPLM Raffaello; Expedition 4 crew exchange; Starshine 2
108. STS-109	Fourth HST servicing
109. STS-110	13th ISS mission, 8A; S0 truss; Mobile Transporter
110. STS-111	14th ISS mission, UF-2; MPLM Leonardo; MBS; Expedition 5 crew exchange
111. STS-112	15th ISS mission, 8A; S1 truss; CETA cart A
112. STS-113	16th ISS mission, 11A; P1 truss
113. STS-107	Research mission; SPACEHAB; Hitchhiker pallet
114. STS-114	17th ISS mission, LF-1, MPLM Raffaello
115. STS-121	18th ISS mission, ULF-1.1; MPLM Leonardo
116. STS-115	19th ISS mission, 12A; P3/P4 truss
117. STS-116	20th ISS mission, 12A.1; P5 truss

APPENDIX B: ASTRONAUTS PAST AND PRESENT*

Astronaut	Mission(s) Flown	Astronaut	Mission(s) Flown
ACTON, Loren W.	STS-51F	BOWERSOX, Kenneth D.	STS-50, STS-61, STS-73, STS-82, STS-113 (up)
ADAMSON, James C.	STS-28, STS-43	BRADY, Charles E., Jr.	STS-78
AKERS, Thomas D.	STS-41, STS-49, STS-61, STS-79	BRAND, Vance D.	Apollo-*Soyuz*, STS-5, STS-41B, STS-35
ALDRIN, Edwin E. "Buzz," Jr.	Gemini XII, Apollo 11	BRANDENSTEIN, Daniel C.	STS-8, STS-51G, STS-32, STS-49
AL-SAUD, Sultan Salman Abdul Aziz	STS-51G	BRIDGES, Roy D.	STS-51F
ALLEN, Andrew M.	STS-46, STS-62, STS-75	BROWN, Curtis L., Jr.	STS-47, STS-66, STS-77, STS-85, STS-95, STS-103
ALLEN, Joseph P.	STS-5, STS-51A	BROWN, David M.	STS-107
ALTMAN, Scott D.	STS-90, STS-106, STS-109	BROWN, Mark N.	STS-28, STS-48
ANDERS, William A.	Apollo 8	BUCHLI, James F.	STS-51C, STS-61A, STS-29, STS-48
ANDERSON, Michael P.	STS-89, STS-107	BUCKEY, Jay C.	STS-90
APT, Jerome "Jay"	STS-37, STS-47, STS-59, STS-79	BUDARIN, Nikolai M.	STS-71 (up), STS-113 (up)
ARMSTRONG, Neil A.	Gemini VIII, Apollo 11	BURBANK, Daniel C.	STS-106, STS-115
ASHBY, Jeffrey S.	STS-93, STS-100, STS-112	BURSCH, Daniel W.	STS-51, STS-68, STS-77, STS-108 (up), STS-111 (down)
BAGIAN, James P.	STS-29, STS-40	CABANA, Robert D.	STS-41, STS-53, STS-65, STS-88
BAKER (-SHULMAN), Ellen	STS-34, STS-50, STS-71	CAMARDA, Charles J.	STS-114
BAKER, Michael A.	STS-43, STS-52, STS-68, STS-81	CAMERON, Kenneth D.	STS-37, STS-56, STS-74
BARRY, Daniel T.	STS-72, STS-96, STS-105	CAREY, Duane G.	STS-109
BARTOE, John-David F.	STS-51F	CARPENTER, M. Scott	Mercury-Atlas 7
BAUDRY, Patrick	STS-51G	CARR, Gerald P.	Skylab 4
BEAN, Alan L.	Apollo 12, Skylab 3	CARTER, Manley L. "Sonny"	STS-33
BLAHA, John E.	STS-29, STS-33, STS-43, STS-58, STS-79 (up), STS-81 (down)	CASPER, John H.	STS-36, STS-54, STS-62, STS-77
BLOOMFIELD, Michael J.	STS-86, STS-97, STS-110	CENKER, Robert J.	STS-61C
BLUFORD, Guion S.	STS-8, STS-61A, STS-39, STS-53	CERNAN, Eugene A.	Gemini IX, Apollo 10, Apollo 17
BOBKO, Karol J.	STS-6, STS-51D, STS-51J	CHAFFEE, Roger B.	Apollo 1**
BOLDEN, Charles F., Jr.	STS-61C, STS-31, STS-45, STS-60	CHANG-DIAZ, Franklin R.	STS-61C, STS-34, STS-46, STS-60, STS-75, STS-91, STS-111
BONDAR, Roberta L.	STS-42	CHAWLA, Kalpana	STS-87, STS-107
BORMAN, Frank	Gemini VII, Apollo 8	CHELI, Maurizio	STS-75

Astronaut	Mission(s) Flown	Astronaut	Mission(s) Flown
CHIAO, Leroy	STS-65, STS-72, STS-92	DUFFY, Brian K.	STS-45, STS-57, STS-72, STS-92
CHILTON, Kevin P.	STS-49, STS-59, STS-76	DUKE, Charles M., Jr.	Apollo 16
CHRÉTIEN, Jean-Loup	STS-86	DUNBAR, Bonnie J.	STS-61A, STS-32, STS-50, STS-71, STS-89
CLARK, Laurel B. S.	STS-107	DUQUE, Pedro	STS-95
CLEAVE, Mary L.	STS-61B, STS-30	DURRANCE, Samuel T.	STS-35, STS-67
CLERVOY, Jean-Francois	STS-66, STS-84, STS-103	EDWARDS, Joe F., Jr.	STS-89
CLIFFORD, Michael R.	STS-53, STS-59, STS-76	EISELE, Donn F.	Apollo 7
COATS, Michael L.	STS-41D, STS-29, STS-39	ENGLAND, Anthony W.	STS-51F
		ENGLE, Joe H.	STS-2, STS-51I
COCKRELL, Kenneth D.	STS-56, STS-69, STS-80, STS-98, STS-111	EVANS, Ronald E.	Apollo 17
		FABIAN, John M.	STS-7, STS-51G
COLEMAN, Catherine G. "Cady"	STS-73, STS-93	FAVIER, Jean-Jacques	STS-78
COLLINS, Eileen M.	STS-63, STS-84, STS-93, STS-114	FERGUSON, Christopher J.	STS-115
		FETTMAN, Martin J.	STS-58
COLLINS, Michael	Gemini X, Apollo 11	FISHER, Anna L.	STS-51A
CONRAD, Charles, "Pete," Jr.	Gemini V, Gemini XI, Apollo 12, Skylab 2	FISHER, William F.	STS-51I
COOPER, L. Gordon, Jr.	Mercury-Atlas 9, Gemini V	FOALE, C. Michael	STS-45, STS-56, STS-63, STS-84 (up), STS-86 (down), STS-103
COVEY, Richard O.	STS-51I, STS-26, STS-38, STS-61		
CREIGHTON, John O.	STS-51G, STS-36, STS-48	FORRESTER, Patrick G.	STS-105
		FOSSUM, Michael E.	STS-121
CRIPPEN, Robert L.	STS-1, STS-7, STS-41C, STS-41G	FRICK, Stephen N.	STS-110
CROUCH, Roger K.	STS-83, STS-94	FRIMOUT, Dirk D. "Dick"	STS-45
		FUGLESANG, Christer	STS-116
CULBERTSON, Frank L., Jr.	STS-38, STS-51, STS-105 (up), STS-108 (down)	FULLERTON, Charles G. "Gordo"	STS-3, STS-51F
CUNNINGHAM, Walter	Apollo 7	FURRER, Reinhard	STS-61A
CURBEAM, Robert L.	STS-85, STS-98, STS-116	GAFFNEY, F. Andrew "Drew"	STS-40
		GARDNER, Dale A.	STS-8, STS-51A
CURRIE (-SHERLOCK), Nancy J.	STS-57, STS-70, STS-88, STS-109	GARDNER, Guy S.	STS-27, STS-35
DAVIS, N. Jan	STS-47, STS-60, STS-85	GARN, E. Jacob	STS-51D
		GARNEAU, Marc	STS-41G, STS-77, STS-97
DELUCAS, Lawrence J.	STS-50	GARRIOTT, Owen K.	Skylab 3, STS-9
DEZHUROV, Vladimir N.	STS-71 (down), STS-105 (up), STS-108 (down)	GEMAR, Charles D. "Sam"	STS-38, STS-48, STS-62
DOI, Takao	STS-87		

Astronaut	Mission(s) Flown
GERNHARDT, Michael L.	STS-69, STS-83, STS-94, STS-104
GIBSON, Edward G.	Skylab 4
GIBSON, Robert L. "Hoot"	STS-41B, STS-61C, STS-27, STS-47, STS-71
GIDZENKO, Yuri P.	STS-102 (down)
GLENN, John H., Jr.	Mercury-Atlas 6, STS-95
GODWIN, Linda M.	STS-37, STS-59, STS-76, STS-108
GORDON, Richard F., Jr.	Gemini XI, Apollo 12
GORIE, Dominic L. P.	STS-91, STS-99, STS-108
GRABE, Ronald J.	STS-51J, STS-30, STS-42, STS-57
GREGORY, Frederick D.	STS-51B, STS-33, STS-44
GREGORY, William G.	STS-67
GRIGGS, Stanley D.	STS-51D
GRISSOM, Virgil I. "Gus"	Mercury-Redstone 3, Gemini III, Apollo 1**
GRUNSFELD, John M.	STS-67, STS-81, STS-103, STS-109
GUIDONI, Umberto	STS-75, STS-100
GUTIERREZ, Sidney M.	STS-40, STS-59
HADFIELD, Chris A.	STS-74, STS-100
HAISE, Fred W., Jr.	Apollo 13
HALSELL, James D., Jr.	STS-65, STS-74, STS-83, STS-94, STS-101
HAMMOND, L. Blaine, Jr.	STS-39, STS-64
HARBAUGH, Gregory J.	STS-39, STS-54, STS-71, STS-82
HARRIS Bernard A., Jr.	STS-55, STS-63
HART, Terry J.	STS-41C
HARTSFIELD, Henry W. "Hank"	STS-4, STS-41D, STS-61A
HAUCK, Frederick "Rick" H.	STS-7, STS-51A, STS-26
HAWLEY, Steven A.	STS-41D, STS-61C, STS-31, STS-82, STS-93

Astronaut	Mission(s) Flown
HELMS, Susan J.	STS-54, STS-64, STS-78, STS-101, STS-102 (up), STS-105 (down)
HENIZE, Karl G.	STS-51F
HENNEN, Thomas J.	STS-44
HENRICKS, Terence T. "Tom"	STS-44, STS-55, STS-70, STS-78
HERRINGTON, John B.	STS-113
HIEB, Richard J.	STS-39, STS-49, STS-65
HIGGINBOTHAM, Joan E.	STS-116
HILMERS, David C.	STS-51J, STS-26, STS-36, STS-42
HIRE, Kathryn P.	STS-90
HOBAUGH, Charles O.	STS-104
HOFFMAN, Jeffrey A.	STS-51D, STS-35, STS-46, STS-61, STS-75
HOROWITZ, Scott J.	STS-75, STS-82, STS-101, STS-105
HUGHES-FULFORD, Millie E.	STS-40
HUSBAND, Rick D.	STS-96, STS-107
IRWIN, James B.	Apollo 15
IVINS, Marsha S.	STS-32, STS-46, STS-62, STS-81, STS-98
JARVIS, Gregory B.	STS-51L
JEMISON, Mae C.	STS-47
JERNIGAN, Tamara E.	STS-40, STS-52, STS-67, STS-80, STS-96
JETT, Brent W., Jr.	STS-72, STS-81, STS-97, STS-115
JONES, Thomas D.	STS-59, STS-68, STS-80, STS-98
KADENYUK, Leonid K.	STS-87
KAVANDI, Janet L.	STS-91, STS-99, STS-104
KELLY, James M.	STS-102, STS-114
KELLY, Mark E.	STS-108, STS-121
KELLY, Scott J.	STS-103
KERWIN, Joseph P.	Skylab 2
KONDAKOVA, Yelena V.	STS-84

Astronaut	Mission(s) Flown
KORZUN, Valery G.	STS-111 (up), STS-113 (down)
KREGEL, Kevin R.	STS-70, STS-78, STS-87, STS-99
KRIKALEV, Sergei K.	STS-60, STS-88, STS-102 (down)
LAWRENCE, Wendy B.	STS-67, STS-86, STS-91, STS-114
LEE, Mark C.	STS-30, STS-47, STS-64, STS-82
LEESTMA, David C.	STS-41G, STS-28, STS-45
LENOIR, William B.	STS-5
LESLIE, Fred W.	STS-73
LICHTENBERG, Byron K.	STS-9, STS-45
LIND, Don L.	STS-51B
LINDSEY, Steven W.	STS-87, STS-95, STS-104, STS-121
LINENGER, Jerry M.	STS-64, STS-81 (up), STS-84 (down)
LINNEHAN, Richard M.	STS-78, STS-90, STS-109
LINTERIS, Gregory T.	STS-83, STS-94
LOCKHART, Paul S.	STS-111, STS-113
LONCHAKOV, Yuri V.	STS-100
LOPEZ-ALEGRIA, Michael E.	STS-73, STS-92, STS-113
LOUNGE, John M. "Mike"	STS-51I, STS-26, STS-35
LOUSMA, Jack R.	Skylab 3, STS-3
LOVELL, James A., Jr.	Gemini VII, Gemini XII, Apollo 8, Apollo 13
LOW, G. David	STS-32, STS-43, STS-57
LU, Edward T.	STS-84, STS-106
LUCID, Shannon W.	STS-51G, STS-34, STS-43, STS-58, STS-76 (up), STS-79 (down)
MACLEAN, Steven G.	STS-52, STS-115
MAGNUS, Sandra H.	STS-112
MALENCHENKO, Yuri I.	STS-106
MALERBA, Franco A.	STS-46
MASSIMINO, Michael J.	STS-109

Astronaut	Mission(s) Flown
MASTRACCHIO, Richard A.	STS-106
MATTINGLY, Thomas K., II	Apollo 16, STS-4, STS-51C
McARTHUR, William S., Jr.	STS-58, STS-74, STS-92
McAULIFFE, Sharon C.	STS-51L
McBRIDE, Jon A.	STS-41G
McCANDLESS, Bruce, II	STS-41B, STS-31
McCOOL, William C.	STS-107
McCULLEY, Michael J.	STS-34
McDIVITT, James A.	Gemini IV, Apollo 9
McMONAGLE, Donald R.	STS-39, STS-54, STS-66
McNAIR, Ronald E.	STS-41B, STS-51L
MEADE, Carl J.	STS-38, STS-50, STS-64
MELNICK, Bruce E.	STS-41, STS-49
MELROY, Pamela A.	STS-92, STS-112
MERBOLD, Ulf D.	STS-9, STS-42
MESSERSCHMID, Ernst W.	STS-61A
MITCHELL, Edgar D.	Apollo 14
MOHRI, Mamoru M.	STS-47, STS-99
MORIN, Lee M. E.	STS-110
MORUKOV, Boris V.	STS-106
MULLANE, Richard M.	STS-41D, STS-27, STS-36
MUSGRAVE, F. Story	STS-6, STS-51F, STS-33, STS-44, STS-61, STS-80
NAGEL, Steven R.	STS-51G, STS-61A, STS-37, STS-55
NAITO-MUKAI, Chiaki H.	STS-65, STS-95
NELSON, C. William "Bill"	STS-61C
NELSON, George D.	STS-41C, STS-61C, STS-26
NEWMAN, James H.	STS-51, STS-69, STS-88, STS-109
NICOLLIER, Claude	STS-46, STS-61, STS-75, STS-103
NOGUCHI, Soichi	STS-114
NORIEGA, Carlos I.	STS-84, STS-97
NOWAK, Lisa M.	STS-121

Astronaut	Mission(s) Flown
O'CONNOR, Bryan D.	STS-61B, STS-40
OCHOA, Ellen	STS-56, STS-66, STS-96, STS-110
OCKELS, Wubbo J.	STS-61A
OEFELEIN, William A.	STS-116
ONIZUKA, Ellison S.	STS-51C, STS-51L
ONUFRIYENKO, Yuriy I.	STS-108 (up), STS-111 (down)
OSWALD, Stephen S.	STS-42, STS-56, STS-67
OVERMYER, Robert F.	STS-5, STS-51B
PAILES, William A.	STS-51J
PARAZYNSKI, Scott E.	STS-66, STS-86, STS-95, STS-100
PARISE, Ronald A.	STS-35, STS-67
PARKER, Robert A. R.	STS-9, STS-35
PATRICK, Nicholas J. M.	STS-116
PAWELCZYK, James A.	STS-90
PAYETTE, Julie	STS-96
PAYTON, Gary E.	STS-51C
PERRIN, Philippe	STS-111
PETERSON, Donald H.	STS-6
PETTIT, Donald	STS-113 (up)
PHILLIPS, John L.	STS-100
POGUE, William R.	Skylab 4
POLANSKY, Mark L.	STS-98, STS-116
PRECOURT, Charles J.	STS-55, STS-71, STS-84, STS-91
RAMON, Ilan	STS-107
READDY, William F.	STS-42, STS-51, STS-79
REIGHTLER, Kenneth S., Jr.	STS-48, STS-60
REILLY, James F.	STS-89, STS-104
REITER, Thomas	STS-121 (up), STS-116 (down)
RESNICK, Judith A.	STS-41D, STS-51L
RICHARDS, Paul W.	STS-102
RICHARDS, Richard N.	STS-28, STS-41, STS-50, STS-64
RIDE, Sally K.	STS-7, STS-41G

Astronaut	Mission(s) Flown
ROBINSON, Stephen K.	STS-85, STS-95, STS-114
ROMINGER, Kent V.	STS-73, STS-80, STS-85, STS-96, STS-100
ROOSA, Stuart A.	Apollo 14
ROSS, Jerry L.	STS-61B, STS-27, STS-37, STS-55, STS-74, STS-88, STS-110
RUNCO, Mario, Jr.	STS-44, STS-54, STS-77
RYUMIN, Valery V.	STS-91
SACCO, Albert, Jr.	STS-73
SCHIRRA, Walter M., Jr.	Mercury-Atlas 8, Gemini VI, Apollo 7
SCHLEGEL, Hans W.	STS-55
SCHMITT, Harrison H. "Jack"	Apollo 17
SCHWEICKART, Russell L. "Rusty"	Apollo 9
SCOBEE, Francis R. "Dick"	STS-41C, STS-51L
SCOTT, David R.	Gemini VIII, Apollo 9, Apollo 15
SCOTT, Winston E.	STS-72, STS-87
SCULLY-POWER, Paul D.	STS-41G
SEARFOSS, Richard A.	STS-58, STS-76, STS-90
SEDDON, Margaret R.	STS-51D, STS-40, STS-58
SEGA, Ronald M.	STS-60, STS-76
SELLERS, Piers J.	STS-112, STS-121
SHARIPOV, Salizhan S.	STS-89
SHAW, Brewster H., Jr.	STS-9, STS-61B, STS-28
SHEPARD, Alan B., Jr.	Mercury-Redstone 3, Apollo 14
SHEPHERD, William M.	STS-27, STS-41, STS-52, STS-102 (down)
SHRIVER, Loren J.	STS-51C, STS-31, STS-46
SLAYTON, Donald K. "Deke"	Apollo-*Soyuz*
SMITH, Michael J.	STS-51L
SMITH, Steven L.	STS-68, STS-82, STS-103, STS-110

Astronaut	Mission(s) Flown
SOLOVYEV, Anatoly Y.	STS-71 (up)
SPRING, Sherwood C. "Woody"	STS-61B
SPRINGER, Robert C.	STS-29, STS-38
STAFFORD, Thomas P., Jr.	Gemini VI, Gemini IX, Apollo 10, Apollo-*Soyuz*
STEFANYSHYN-PIPER, Heidemarie	STS-115
STEWART, Robert L.	STS-41B, STS-51J
STILL Susan L.	STS-83, STS-94
STREKALOV, Gennady M.	STS-71 (down)
STURCKOW, Frederick W. "Rick"	STS-88, STS-105
SULLIVAN, Kathryn D.	STS-41G, STS-31, STS-45
SWIGERT, John L. "Jack," Jr.	Apollo 13
TANI, Daniel M.	STS-108
TANNER, Joseph R.	STS-66, STS-82, STS-97, STS-115
THAGARD, Norman E.	STS-7, STS-51B, STS-30, STS-42, STS-71 (down)
THIELE, Gerhard P. J.	STS-99
THIRSK, Robert B.	STS-78
THOMAS, Andrew S. W.	STS-77, STS-89 (up), STS-91 (down), STS-102, STS-114
THOMAS, Donald A.	STS-65, STS-70, STS-83, STS-94
THORNTON, Kathryn C.	STS-33, STS-49, STS-61, STS-73
THORNTON, William E.	STS-8, STS-51B
THUOT, Pierre J.	STS-36, STS-49, STS-62
TITOV, Vladimir G.	STS-63, STS-86
TOGNINI, Michel	STS-93
TOKAREV, Valery I.	STS-96
TRESCHEV, Sergei Y.	STS-111 (up), STS-113 (down)
TRINH, Eugene H.	STS-50
TRULY, Richard H.	STS-2, STS-8
TRYGGVASON, Bjarni V.	STS-85

Astronaut	Mission(s) Flown
TYURIN, Mikhail V.	STS-105 (up), STS-108 (down)
USACHEV, Yury V.	STS-101, STS-102 (up), STS-105 (down)
VAN DEN BERG, Lodewijk	STS-51B
VAN HOFTEN, James D.	STS-41C, STS-51I
VEACH, Charles L.	STS-39, STS-52
VELA, Rodolfo N.	STS-61B
VOSS, James S.	STS-44, STS-53, STS-69, STS-101, STS-102 (up), STS-105 (down)
VOSS, Janice E.	STS-57, STS-63, STS-83, STS-94, STS-99
WAKATA, Koicho	STS-72, STS-92
WALHEIM, Rex J.	STS-110
WALKER, Charles D.	STS-41D, STS-51D, STS-61B
WALKER, David M.	STS-51A, STS-30, STS-53, STS-69
WALTER, Ulrich	STS-55
WALZ, Carl E.	STS-51, STS-65, STS-79, STS-108 (up), STS-111 (down)
WANG, Taylor G.	STS-51B
WEBER, Mary E.	STS-70, STS-101
WEITZ, Paul J.	Skylab 2, STS-6
WETHERBEE, James D.	STS-32, STS-52, STS-63, STS-86, STS-102, STS-113
WHITE, Edward H., II	Gemini IV, Apollo 1**
WHITSON, Peggy	STS-111 (up), STS-113 (down)
WILCUTT, Terrence W.	STS-68, STS-79, STS-89, STS-106
WILLIAMS, Dafydd R.	STS-90
WILLIAMS, Donald E.	STS-51D, STS-34
WILLIAMS, Jeffrey N.	STS-101
WILLIAMS, Sunita L.	STS-116
WILSON, Stephanie D.	STS-121
WISOFF, Peter J. K. "Jeff"	STS-57, STS-68, STS-81, STS-92

Astronaut	Mission(s) Flown
WOLF, David A.	STS-58, STS-86 (up), STS-89 (down), STS-112
WORDEN, Alfred M.	Apollo 15
YOUNG, John W.	Gemini III, Gemini X, Apollo 10, Apollo 16, STS-1, STS-9
YURCHIKHIN, Fyodor N.	STS-112

* Note: In this table, the term "astronaut" refers to all individuals, U.S. and non-U.S. astronauts, who have flown aboard U.S. space missions (Mercury, Gemini, Apollo, Skylab, Apollo-*Soyuz*, and Space Shuttle) with the exception of Roger Chaffee, member of the Apollo 1 crew, who also is mentioned. Expedition crews that have flown to the International Space Station are not necessarily included in this list, as some crew members have been launched and returned to Earth aboard Russian Soyuz launch vehicles. Please turn to the ISS section for more information regarding ISS Expedition crews.

** Died on the launchpad. Apollo 1 is not technically a spaceflight.

Useful Web Site:
http://www.jsc.nasa.gov/Bios/ (Astronaut Biographies)

APPENDIX C: Acronyms

ACCESS: Assembly Concept for Construction of Erectable Space Structures

ACS: Advanced Camera for Survey

ACTS: Advanced Communications Technology Satellite

AEB: Agência Espacial Brasileira (Brazilian Space Agency)

AMU: Astronaut Maneuvering Unit

ASI: Agenzia Spaziale Italiana (Italian Space Agency)

ASTP: Apollo-*Soyuz* Test Project

ASTRO-SPAS: Astronomical SPAS

ATDA: Augmented Target Docking Adapter

ATLAS: Atmospheric Laboratory for Applications and Science

ATM: Apollo Telescope Mount

ATV: Automated Transfer Vehicle

AXAF: Advanced X-ray Astronomy Facility (now Chandra)

CANEX: Canadian Experiment

Cdr: Commander

CDT: Central Daylight Time

CETA: Crew and Equipment Translation Aid

CFES: Continuous Flow Electrophoresis System

CM: Command Module; Combustion Module

CNES: Centre National d'Études Spatiales (French Space Agency)

COCULT: Coculture

COSTAR: Corrective Optics Space Telescope Axial Replacement

CRISTA-SPAS: Cryogenic Infrared Spectrometers and Telescopes for the Atmosphere-SPAS

CSA: Canadian Space Agency

CSM: Command and Service Module

CUE: Central Unit Electronics

DARA: Deutsche Agentur fur Raumfahrtangelegenheiten (German Space Agency)

DOD: Department of Defense

DSP: Defense Support Program

DTO: Development Test Objective

DXS: Diffuse X-Ray Spectrometer

EAS: Early Ammonia Servicer

EASE: Experimental Assembly of Structures in Extravehicular Activity

ECUs: Electronic Control Units

EDO: Extended Duration Orbiter

EDT: Eastern Daylight Time

ERBS: Earth Radiation Budget Satellite

ESA: European Space Agency

ESC: Electronic Still Camera

ET: External Tank

EURECA: European Retrievable Carrier

EVA: Extravehicular Activity

FARE: Fluid Acquisition and Resupply Equipment

FGB: Functional Cargo Block

FOC: Faint Object Camera

FPP: Floating Potential Probes

GAS: Get-Away Special

GRO: Gamma Ray Observatory

HGA: High-Gain Antenna

HHSMU: Hand-Held Self-Maneuvering Unit

HOST: Hubble Orbiting Systems Test

HST: Hubble Space Telescope

IAE: Inflatable Antenna Experiment

IBSS: Infrared Background Signature Satellite

ICC: Integrated Cargo Carrier

IML: International Microgravity Laboratory

IRIS: Italian Research Interim Stage

ISAC: Interaction of Structures, Aerodynamics, and Controls

ISS: International Space Station

IUS: Inertial Upper Stage

JAXA: Japan Aerospace Exploration Agency (Japanese Space Agency, formerly NASDA)

JPL: Jet Propulsion Laboratory

LAGEOS: Laser Geodynamic Satellite

LDEF: Long Duration Exposure Facility

LF: Logistics Flight

LITE: Lidar In-Space Technology Experiment

LM: Lunar Module

LMS: Life and Microgravity Spacelab

MBS: Mobile Remote Service Base System

MAHRSI: Middle Atmosphere High Resolution Spectrograph Instrument

MISSE: Materials International Space Station Experiment

MIT: Massachusetts Institute of Technology

MMU: Manned Maneuvering Unit

MPLM: Multi-Purpose Logistics Module

MS: Mission Specialist

MSL: Microgravity Science Laboratory

NASDA: National Space and Development Agency (Japanese Space Agency, now JAXA)

NICMOS: Near-Infrared Camera and Multi-Object Spectrometer

NSAU: National Space Agency of Ukraine

OAST: Office of Aeronautics and Space Technology

OBSS: Orbiter Boom Sensor System

ODERACS: Orbital Debris Radar Calibration System

OMS: Orbital Maneuvering System

ORFEUS-SPAS: Orbiting and Retrievable Far and Extreme Ultraviolet Spectrograph-SPAS

OSS: Office of Space Science

OSTA: Office of Space and Terrestrial Applications

OV: Orbital Vehicle

P: Port (i.e., Port 1, P6, etc.)

PAL: Protuberance Air Load

PAM: Payload Assist Module

PC: Payload Commander

PLB: Payload Bay

PMA: Pressurized Mating Adaptor

PS: Payload Specialist

RCC: Reinforced Carbon-Carbon

RCS: Reaction Control System

RDM: Research Double Module

RMS: Remote Manipulator System

RSA: Russian Space Agency

RSC Energia: Rocket & Space Corporation Energia, Russia

RSUs: Rate Sensor Units

RWA: Reaction Wheel Assembly

S: Starboard (i.e., S1 or Starboard 1 truss)

S0: Starboard-Zero Truss

SA: Solar Array

SBS-C: Satellite Business Systems C

SAFER: Simplified Aid for EVA Rescue

SAMS: Space Acceleration Measurement System

SAREX: Shuttle Amateur Radio Experiment

SDI: Strategic Defense Initiative

SESAM: Surface Effects Sample Monitor

SFU: Space Flyer Unit

SHARE: Space Station Heat Pipe Advanced Radiator Element

SLS: Spacelab Life Sciences

Solar Max: Solar Maximum Mission

SPARTAN: Shuttle Pointed Autonomous Research Tool for Astronomy

SPAS: Shuttle Pallet Satellite

SPS: Service Propulsion System

SRB: Solid Rocket Booster

SRL: Space Radar Laboratory

SRTM: Shuttle Radar Topography Mission

SSBUV: Shuttle Solar Backscatter Ultraviolet

SSME: Space Shuttle Main Engine

SSRMS: Space Station Remote Manipulator System

STIS: Space Telescope Imaging Spectrograph

STS: Space Transportation System

TAS: Technology Applications and Science

TEAMS: Technology Experiments for Advancing Mission in Space

TDRS: Tracking and Data Relay Satellites

TMA: Transportnyi (transport) Modifitsirovannyi (modified) Antropometricheskii (anthropometric)

TOS: Transfer Orbit Stage

TSS: Tethered Satellite System

UARS: Upper Atmosphere Research Satellite

UF: Utilization Flight

UHF: ultrahigh frequency

ULF: Utilization and Logistics Flight

USML: U.S. Microgravity Laboratory

USMP: U.S. Microgravity Payload

WSF: Wake Shield Facility

X-SAR: X-band Synthetic Aperture Radar

Z1: Zenith 1

MONOGRAPHS IN AEROSPACE HISTORY

(Most available from *http://history.nasa.gov/series95.html*)

Launius, Roger D., and Aaron K. Gillette, comps. *Toward a History of the Space Shuttle: An Annotated Bibliography.* Monographs in Aerospace History, No. 1, 1992.

Launius, Roger D., and J. D. Hunley, comps. *An Annotated Bibliography of the Apollo Program.* Monographs in Aerospace History, No. 2, 1994.

Launius, Roger D. *Apollo: A Retrospective Analysis.* Monographs in Aerospace History, No. 3, 1994.

Hansen, James R. *Enchanted Rendezvous: John C. Houbolt and the Genesis of the Lunar-Orbit Rendezvous Concept.* Monographs in Aerospace History, No. 4, 1995.

Gorn, Michael H. *Hugh L. Dryden's Career in Aviation and Space.* Monographs in Aerospace History, No. 5, 1996.

Powers, Sheryll Goecke. *Women in Flight Research at NASA Dryden Flight Research Center from 1946 to 1995.* Monographs in Aerospace History, No. 6, 1997.

Portree, David S. F., and Robert C. Trevino. *Walking to Olympus: An EVA Chronology.* Monographs in Aerospace History, No. 7, 1997.

Logsdon, John M., moderator. *Legislative Origins of the National Aeronautics and Space Act of 1958: Proceedings of an Oral History Workshop.* Monographs in Aerospace History, No. 8, 1998.

Rumerman, Judy A., comp. *U.S. Human Spaceflight, A Record of Achievement 1961–1998.* Monographs in Aerospace History, No. 9, 1998.

Portree, David S. F. *NASA's Origins and the Dawn of the Space Age.* Monographs in Aerospace History, No. 10, 1998.

Logsdon, John M. *Together in Orbit: The Origins of International Cooperation in the Space Station.* Monographs in Aerospace History, No. 11, 1998.

Phillips, W. Hewitt. *Journey in Aeronautical Research: A Career at NASA Langley Research Center.* Monographs in Aerospace History, No. 12, 1998.

Braslow, Albert L. *A History of Suction-Type Laminar-Flow Control with Emphasis on Flight Research.* Monographs in Aerospace History, No. 13, 1999.

Logsdon, John M., moderator. *Managing the Moon Program: Lessons Learned From Apollo.* Monographs in Aerospace History, No. 14, 1999.

Perminov, V. G. *The Difficult Road to Mars: A Brief History of Mars Exploration in the Soviet Union.* Monographs in Aerospace History, No. 15, 1999.

Maisel, Martin, Demo J. Giulanetti, and Daniel C. Dugan. *The History of the XV-15 Tilt Rotor Research Aircraft: From Concept to Flight.* Monographs in Aerospace History, No. 17, 2000 (NASA SP-2000-4517).

Jenkins, Dennis R. *Hypersonics Before the Shuttle: A Concise History of the X-15 Research Airplane.* Monographs in Aerospace History, No. 18, 2000 (NASA SP-2000-4518).

Chambers, Joseph R. *Partners in Freedom: Contributions of the Langley Research Center to U.S. Military Aircraft of the 1990s.* Monographs in Aerospace History, No. 19, 2000 (NASA SP-2000-4519).

Waltman, Gene L. *Black Magic and Gremlins: Analog Flight Simulations at NASA's Flight Research Center.* Monographs in Aerospace History, No. 20, 2000 (NASA SP-2000-4520).

Portree, David S. F. *Humans to Mars: Fifty Years of Mission Planning, 1950–2000.* Monographs in Aerospace History, No. 21, 2001 (NASA SP-2001-4521).

Thompson, Milton O., with J. D. Hunley. *Flight Research: Problems Encountered and What They Should Teach Us.* Monographs in Aerospace History, No. 22, 2001 (NASA SP-2001-4522).

Tucker, Tom. *The Eclipse Project.* Monographs in Aerospace History, No. 23, 2001 (NASA SP-2001-4523).

Siddiqi, Asif A. *Deep Space Chronicle: A Chronology of Deep Space and Planetary Probes 1958–2000.* Monographs in Aerospace History, No. 24, 2002 (NASA SP-2002-4524).

Merlin, Peter W. *Mach 3+: NASA/USAF YF-12 Flight Research, 1969–1979.* Monographs in Aerospace History, No. 25, 2001 (NASA SP-2001-4525).

Anderson, Seth B. *Memoirs of an Aeronautical Engineer: Flight Tests at Ames Research Center: 1940–1970.* Monographs in Aerospace History, No. 26, 2002 (NASA SP-2002-4526).

Renstrom, Arthur G. *Wilbur and Orville Wright: A Bibliography Commemorating the One-Hundredth Anniversary of the First Powered Flight on December 17, 1903.* Monographs in Aerospace History, No. 27, 2002 (NASA SP-2002-4527).

No Monograph 28.

Chambers, Joseph R. *Concept to Reality: Contributions of the NASA Langley Research Center to U.S. Civil Aircraft of the 1990s.* Monographs in Aerospace History, No. 29, 2003 (SP-2003-4529).

Peebles, Curtis, ed. *The Spoken Word: Recollections of Dryden History, The Early Years.* Monographs in Aerospace History, No. 30, 2003 (SP-2003-4530).

Jenkins, Dennis R., Tony Landis, and Jay Miller. *American X-Vehicles: An Inventory—X-1 to X-50.* Monographs in Aerospace History, No. 31, 2003 (SP-2003-4531).

Renstrom, Arthur G. *Wilbur and Orville Wright: A Chronology Commemorating the One-Hundredth Anniversary of the First Powered Flight on December 17, 1903.* Monographs in Aerospace History, No. 32, 2002 (NASA SP-2003-4532).

Bowles, Mark D., and Robert S. Arrighi. *NASA's Nuclear Frontier: The Plum Brook Research Reactor.* Monographs in Aerospace History, No. 33, 2003 (SP-2004-4533).

Matranga, Gene J., C. Wayne Ottinger, Calvin R. Jarvis, and D. Christian Gelzer. *Unconventional, Contrary, and Ugly: The Lunar Landing Research Vehicle.* Monographs in Aerospace History, No. 35, 2006 (NASA SP-2006-4535).

McCurdy, Howard E. *Low Cost Innovation in Spaceflight: The History of the Near Earth Asteroid Rendezvous (NEAR) Mission.* Monographs in Aerospace History, No. 36 (NASA SP-2005-4536).

Seamans, Robert C., Jr. *Project Apollo: The Tough Decisions.* Monographs in Aerospace History, No. 37 (NASA SP-2005-4537).

Lambright, W. Henry. *NASA and the Environment: The Case of Ozone Depletion.* Monographs in Aerospace History, No. 38 (NASA SP-2005-4538).

Chambers, Joseph R. *Innovation in Flight: Research of the NASA Langley Research Center on Revolutionary Advanced Concepts for Aeronautics.* Monographs in Aerospace History, No. 39 (NASA SP-2005-4539)

Phillips, W. Hewitt. *Journey Into Space Research: Continuation of a Career at NASA Langley Research Center.* Monographs in Aerospace History, No. 40. (NASA SP-2005-4540).

On 20 July 1969, after a four-day trip, the Apollo 11 astronauts arrived at the Moon. This photo of Earth rising over the lunar horizon taken from the orbiting Command Module is one of the most famous images returned from the space program, although even the astronauts themselves cannot remember who actually took the picture. (AS11-44-6552)

Mission specialist Bruce McCandless II ventured further away from the confines and safety of his ship than any previous astronaut ever had. This space first was made possible by the Manned Manuevering Unit (MMU), a nitrogen-jet-propelled backpack. After a series of test maneuvers inside and above *Challenger*'s payload bay, McCandless went "free-flying" to a distance of 320 feet away from the orbiter. The MMU is controlled by joysticks positioned at the ends of the armrests. Moving the joysticks left or right or by pulling them fires nitrogen jet thrusters propelling McCandless in any direction he chooses. A still camera is mounted on the upper right portion of the MMU. This stunning view shows McCandless with the MMU amongst the black and blue of Earth and space. (S84-27017)